William Emery Barnes

An Apparatus Criticus to Chronicles in the Peshitta Version

William Emery Barnes

An Apparatus Criticus to Chronicles in the Peshitta Version

ISBN/EAN: 9783744661003

Printed in Europe, USA, Canada, Australia, Japan

Cover: Foto ©Thomas Meinert / pixelio.de

More available books at **www.hansebooks.com**

AN
APPARATUS CRITICUS

TO

CHRONICLES IN
THE PESHITTA VERSION

WITH

A DISCUSSION OF THE VALUE OF THE
CODEX AMBROSIANUS

BY

W. E. BARNES, D.D.
FELLOW OF PETERHOUSE,
FORMERLY LECTURER AT CLARE COLLEGE.

CAMBRIDGE:
AT THE UNIVERSITY PRESS.
1897

[*All Rights reserved.*]

Cambridge:
PRINTED BY J. AND C. F. CLAY,
AT THE UNIVERSITY PRESS.

IN PIAM MEMORIAM

BRIANI WALTONI

DOMÛS DIVINI PETRI

OLIM SOCII

PREFACE.

AT the present time the only existing Apparatus Criticus to the Peshitta is the work of Herbert Thorndike in Volume VI. of the London Polyglot of 1657. For Chronicles Thorndike cites two MSS. only, viz., Poc. 391 and Bodl. 141 both of the Seventeenth Century and of the same type of text. Yet since the printed text is derived from a MS. equally late in date and poorer in text, even such an Apparatus is useful. I gratefully acknowledge the help which it has given in the compilation of the present work.

But 240 years have passed since Thorndike published his collations, and time has brought to light MSS. of the Peshitta far older than his. For the present Apparatus two MSS. of the Sixth Century, one of the Ninth, and one of the Twelfth have been used. Moreover for the first time for the book of Chronicles a Nestorian or East Syrian MS. has been within reach.

It is not necessary to say much of the later Jacobite MSS. which are cited for the first time in these pages, or of the fuller citation here of later Jacobite MSS. already known. Such MSS. may probably all be correctly described *either* as poor relations (if not descendants) of the Buchanan Bible, *or* as transcripts of the Florentine MS., *or* as partly one partly the other. They have freely furnished me with specimen-readings, but future editors of the Peshitta text of most books of the Old Testament will, I believe, as a rule dispense with the services of these MSS.

This Apparatus lays no claim to completeness; it does not attempt to register all the variants even of the five primary MSS. It is incomplete also on another side, for it does not appeal to the authority of the Arabic version or of Patristic quotations. The Arabic version indeed does promise help[1], but it must be edited before it can be used. Patristic quotations on the contrary are unpromising. Aphraates and Ephraim have references, but vague ones; Ephraim moreover can be used for the most part in an uncritical edition only. Bar-Hebraeus is late and the source of his quotations (Peshitta, LXX., Hebrew original) is frequently uncertain. Philoxenus (*Discourses*) seems to have no references. Such evidence as I have collected from the Fathers does not seem to be worth printing.

But if the treatment of the text of Chronicles be incomplete, it is hoped that this book will by way of compensation contribute a little towards the textual criticism of the Peshitta in general. Three important questions are directly or indirectly touched on, viz., the value of the Codex Ambrosianus, the source of the characteristic readings of the printed text, and the relation of the Urumia edition (1852) to Nestorian authorities.

It is not easy to acknowledge at all adequately the help and sympathy which scholars both within and without the United Kingdom have given me. Let me first thank Professor Bevan, whose advice, given at an early stage of my work, proved most valuable. To Professor Gwynn of Dublin, Professor D. H. Müller of Vienna, and Mr Gwilliam of Oxford I owe many thanks for

---

[1] In 1 Chr. IV. 9 it agrees with Codd. AC (*wa-qāra maḥbūban min ummihi wa-abihi*).

PREFACE.

their courteous replies to the enquiries of a stranger. Professor Sachau of Berlin most kindly collated MS. "Sachau 90" in three important passages for me. Professor Guidi of Rome to whom, though I was a stranger, I ventured to apply for half-a-dozen readings from Codd. d m r v, most generously sent me readings from these MSS. covering the first six chapters of Chronicles. These readings are given in the Apparatus; rightly they should be marked d^g m$^{\prime g}$ r^g v^g.

My heaviest debt of thanks remains to be paid. Dr Ceriani of Milan has always been generous to scholars who apply to him for help; my own experience has been no whit behind that of others. He it was who called my attention to the two important MSS. F and s. He allowed me to use his own collation of s with A in the books of Chronicles,—a most generous permission. He gave me introductions which greatly smoothed my course in Rome. Perhaps the greatest boon of all was the sympathy shewn by a Veteran Scholar for a novice's work. My heartiest thanks are due to Dr Ceriani.

I desire also to acknowledge the courteous assistance given me at the following Libraries, the Cambridge University Library, the Bodleian, the British Museum, the Bibliothèque Nationale, the Ambrosian Library at Milan, the Laurentian at Florence, the Royal Library at Berlin, the Vatican Library and the Library of the Propaganda at Rome. At Rome I desire particularly to acknowledge the kindness of Father Ehrle, Monsignor Ugolini, and Signor Durantini.

To the Syndics of the Cambridge University Press I offer my heartiest thanks for undertaking the publication of this book, and to the staff of the Press for the care bestowed on the printing of it.

One last word remains to be said. I have challenged in the Introduction a view put forward by Professor Cornill in 1886; I am glad to know on the best authority that I do not thereby challenge the Professor Cornill of to-day. In a letter (dated May 24) written in a most generous tone he tells me that he has changed his view "schon seit Rahlfs" (i.e. Rahlfs' article, "Beiträge zur Textkritik der Peschita," ZATW 1889, pp. 161 —210). It is a great pleasure to me that this book thereby loses whatever controversial character it originally had.

A brief answer may be given here to the question, What on the whole is the result of a comparison of the printed text of Chronicles with the best MSS. at present known. The answer may be given under four heads.

(*a*) The text is augmented by the addition of several clauses and of a passage of fifty-four verses (I. XXVI. 13—XXVII. 34) previously omitted.

(*b*) Two or three clauses have to be omitted.

(*c*) The text remains corrupt in several places.

(*d*) The Midrashic euphemistic and paraphrastic character of several passages remains unaffected.

(*a*) The clauses which must probably be restored to the text occur as follows:—

I. IV. 24; V. 23; XVI. 10; XVII. 2, 4; XXI. 17; XXIX. 11, 18.

II. III. 8; IV. 8; VI. 32; X. 17; XXII. 6; XXVIII. 18, 23; XXIX. 22, 23; XXX. 2; XXXI. 1; XXXII. 14, 17.

(*b*) For clauses which must be omitted see:—

I. XVIII. 7; XX. 4, 5; II. IX. 12.

(*c*) Corruptions for which the MSS. supply no remedy occur:—

I. II. 18 (ܝܗܕ for ܐܗܕܐ?); II. XXVIII. 7 (ܠܚܕܝ, for ܐܚܕܝ?).

(*d*) Striking passages containing characteristic renderings which remain unaffected by an appeal to MSS. are the following:

I. IV. 9. "[His father] called his name 'My eyes' (Heb. 'Jabez')." So ABCF s[b].

V. 2. "From Judah shall proceed ("hath proceeded" F) King Messiah" (Heb. 'Of him—Judah—one became ruler'). So ABC [F] s[b]. Cod. d[1] stands alone in reading: ܘܡܢܗܘ ܢܓܒܪ ܗܘܐ ܡܫܝܚܐ ܡܠܟܐ, ܕܡܢܗ ܢܦܩܘ ܗܘܘ ܟܠܗܘܢ.

12. "And Joel went forth at their head and judged them and taught them the Scriptures well" (Heb. יואל הראש ושפט המשנה). So ABCF s[b].

VII. 21 b (Heb.) is represented simply by the words, "The men the sons of Gath who were born in the land came down to take their cattle." Thus the Peshitta (so ABCF s[b]) represents the raid as carried out by the Gittites against the Ephraimites, reversing the statement of the original.

XII. 1. The paraphrastic rendering of this verse is confirmed by ABCF s[cer]. "All these mighty men of David were with him in war, and these entered in with David into the city of Ziklag when he fled from the presence of Saul the son of Kish; and they in their might were all servants (so BC, "men" AF) of David; and if he had been willing, they would have killed Saul the son of Kish, for they were mighty men, and the men were warriors; and David was not willing to allow them to kill Saul."

XXII. 12. "And he shall give thee wisdom and *prophecy*." So AB s[b]. [hiant CF] Not so Targum.

XXIX. 15. "For we are made like the smoke of the pot, and we sojourn with thee and are of small account in the world; and thou didst rule over our fathers of old and thou didst command them in what way they should go that they might live."

"For we sojourn with thee and are strangers as all our

---

[1] Written by Sergius Risius, Archbishop of Damascus, † A.D. 1638.

fathers; as the shadow of a bird that flieth in the air of heaven, so is our day upon earth, and there is no hope for a man that he will live for ever" (Targ.).

II. VIII. 14. "David...who rose up in the kingdom before the Lord." So ABCF s^b. "David the prophet of the Lord" (Targ.)   "David the man of God" (Heb.).

XXI. 10. "Then the Edomites who dwelt in Libnah rebelled." So ABCF s^b. "Then Libnah rebelled" (Heb. Targ.).

XXI. 11. "And he gave the Nazirites of Jerusalem wine to drink." So ABCF s^b. "And he caused the inhabitants of Jerusalem to commit fornication" (Heb.). "And he caused the inhabitants of Jerusalem to err" (Targ.).

XXIV. 22. "And his *sons* (the sons of Jehoiada) when *they* were put to death said" etc. So ABC s^b.

XXVIII. 23—25. The strange transposition of these verses is supported by ABCF s^b. (In the apparatus criticus the Hebrew order of verses has been given.)

XXXII. 31. "And he sought the law of the Lord, as it was given him in the land; and he knew all that was in his heart." So ABF s^{cer}. "And thus in the business of the ambassadors of the princes of the king of Babylon who were sent to him to enquire of the wonder which was in the land, to see the two tables of stone which were in the ark of the covenant of the Lord, which Moses deposited there with the two tables of stone which were broken because of the sin of the calf which they made in Horeb, the Word of the Lord gave him licence to shew them (and he was not injured) in order to try him, to know all that was in his heart" (Targ.).

XXXIII. 7. "And he put the image of four faces which he had made in the house of the Lord." So ABF s^b. Cp. Talm. Bab. Sanhed. 103 b: "פֶּסֶל is written (i.e. in *v.* 7) and again פְּסִילִים is written (i.e. in *v.* 19). R. Johanan said: At the beginning he made for it one face, and at the end he made for it four faces, so that the Shekinah might see it and be grieved."[1] "And he set up the graven image of the form which he had made in his own likeness (בדיוקניה *si sana sit lectio*) in the sanctuary of the Lord" (Targ.).

XXXV. 23. "Pharaoh the Lame shot Josiah *with two arrows.*" So ABF s[b]. "The archers shot arrows at king Josiah" (Targ.).

The most striking feature however of the Peshitta version of Chronicles in *GIVLU* is the substitution of 1 Kings XII. 25 —30 followed by 1 Kings XIV. 1—9 for 2 Chron. XI. 5—XII. 12. This substitution has the support of Codd. ABCF s[b] and must therefore be accepted as a feature of the original text. This important fact should make the critic pause before rejecting readings simply because they have been to all appearance introduced from some parallel passage. The Peshitta version of Chronicles appears in the printed editions as a freely altered text; an appeal to the best MSS. within our reach suggests that the alterations belong to the original form of the version.

W. E. B.

---

[1] Joseph Perles, *Meletemata Peschitthoniana*, p. 16.

ADDENDA.

(s = readings of "Sachau 90" collated by Professor E. C. Sachau.)

II. Chron. II. 14 [13]. We may trace the growth of variation as follows:—

    ܘܒܢ̈ܬܗܘܢ ܠܗܘܢ ܘܢܫ̈ܝܗܘܢ ܠܗܘܢ   A.

    ܘܒܢ̈ܬܗܘܢ   ,,   ,,   s^s (sine ܠܗܘܢ 2do) 𝔇𝔊.

    ,,   ܒܢ̈ܬܗܘܢ   F (sine ܠܗܘܢ utroque).

    ,,   ܒܢ̈ܬܗܘܢ ܥܡ   B (so GWLU).

II. Chron. XV. 17.   ܒܩܪܝܬ ܠܗܘܢ   GWLU = BC   s^s 𝔇𝔊.

     ܡܘܠܕܬ ܠܗܘܢ   F.

XVI. 12. ܘܐܬܩܢܘ (sine add.) GWLU = B.

Add. ܡܢ ܐܝܟ ܠܗܘܢ (ut 3 Reg. XV. 23, ABN) F s^s 𝔇𝔊.

INTRODUCTION.

§ 1. *Printed Editions.*

THE Peshitta text of I. II. Chronicles has been printed five times. The editio princeps is that of the Paris Polyglot of 1645 (cited in these pages as *G*) which was reproduced without any improvements in the London Polyglot of 1657 (cited as *W*). In 1823 Lee reproduced again the text of *G*, omitting the vowels, introducing about half a dozen better readings (I. XVI. 1, 43; XXI. 22; II. V. 9; XXIII. 18) and about half a dozen misprints (I. V. 25; XXI. 17; II. V. 6, 9, 14; VII. 10). It will be seen moreover from a list of readings given below that Lee rejected or neglected better readings even in cases in which his own three MSS. (the "Buchanan Bible" and the two Oxford codices) agree against the readings of *G*. His edition is here cited as *L*. The edition (cited as *U*) printed at Urumia by the American missionaries in 1852 is a reproduction of *L* in Nestorian characters with Nestorian vowels and with improved spellings. Some of Lee's misprints are corrected, but no variation from *L* may be safely reckoned as a various reading based on manuscript authority. Thus the four editions of the books of Chronicles are but for Lee's half-dozen improvements reducible to one edition; so that except in these half-dozen places *G*, the editio princeps, represents the present state of the printed text. The fifth issue is dated "Mosul, 1887," but I have not been able to see it, nor does it seem, judged by the reports of those who have seen it, to have any independent value.

Most unfortunately *G*, the editio princeps, was printed from MS. "Syriaques 6" of the Bibliothèque Nationale, a MS. of less value than any other which I have examined. "Syriaques 6" (cited here as "z") was unfortunate both in its birth and in its bringing up. From the first it contained more errors due to homœoteleuton than any other of the MSS. here cited; and it was afterwards revised by an editor[1] who made corrections in the text and supplied omissions in the margin on a large scale often without any manuscript authority whatsoever. The editorial readings in z frequently stand, as will presently be shewn, absolutely alone. I have cited these readings whether occurring in the text or in the margin with z^2. Through G many of them have passed not only into W and L, but also into U.

The two tables following illustrate the dependence of the printed editions on z and on z^2. (The sign > should be read "against the authority of".)

I.

$GW[LU] = z >$ all other authorities examined.

I. VI. 49*†	$GWLU$	$>$ ABCF	d e m p r s^b u v
XIII. 6*†	„	$>$ BCF	a e p r s^{cer} u v
XVI. 1	GW	$>$ BF	a e p r s^b u v [AC hiant]
„ 39*†	$GWLU$	$>$ BF	a e p r s^b u v [AC hiant]
„ 43	GW	$>$ B[F]	a e p r s^b u v [AC hiant]
XXI. 17*†	$GWLU$	$>$ ABC	a e p r s^b u v [F hiat]
„ 22	GW	$>$ ABC	a d e m p r s^b u [F hiat]
XXIX. 18*†	$GWLU$	$>$ ABF	a e p r s^b u v [C hiat]
II. VII. 14*†	„	$>$ ABCF	e p r s^b u v
IX. 1*†	„	$>$ ABCF	e p r s^b u v
X. 17*†	„	$>$ ABCF	e l p r [s^b] u v
XIV. 11*†	„	$>$ BCF	e p r [s^b] u v [A hiat]
XXV. 16*	GWL	$>$ ABCF	e l p r s^b u v

---

[1] Zotenberg (Catalogue, p. 2) strangely identifies this editor with [E.] Renaudot (born 1646), while (rightly) asserting that this MS. was used for the Paris Polyglot of 1645. It is clear that z was edited for the press, and that the editor's notation corresponds with the notation of the folios and columns of G.

INTRODUCTION. xvii

XXVIII. 9   *GW*   > ABCF   e p r s^b u v
  „   23*† *GWLU* > ABCF   e l p r s^h u v
XXXII. 17*†   „   > ABF   a e p r s^b u v [C hiat]
  „   32*   *GWL*   > ABF   e l p r s^{cer} u v [C hiat]
XXXIII. 17*† *GWLU* > ABF   l p r s^b u v [C hiat]
XXXIV. 17*†   „   > ABF   e p r s^b u v [C hiat]

II.

(*GWL*[*U*] = z^2 > all other authorities examined.)

I. 1. 7* ܡܘܪܐܪܐ *GWL* > [A]BCF   d e m p r s^b u v
   IV. 9*† ܚܡܐ *GWLU* > ABCF   a d e l m p r s^{cer} u v
   V. 1*† ܪܚܡܪܚ ܪܐܒܐ *GWLU* > ABCF   a d e l m p r s^b u v
   VI. 55*† ܣܚܙܐ *GWLU* > ABCF   a d e m p r s^b u v z^1
   XI. 3*† ܩܨܐ *GWLU* > [A]BC[F]   a e p r s^{cer} u [hiant v z^1]
   „ 17*† ܕܘܚܪܢ *GWLU* > ABCF   a e p r s^b u v z$^{1\,at\,vid}$
   XII. 1*† ܪܐܪܪ ,ܡܐܙܪܡ *GWLU* > [A]BC[F]   a e p r s^{cer} u v z^1
   XIII. 7*† ܪܐܠܝܠ *GWLU* > BCF   a e p r s^b u v [hiat A]
   „ 13*† ܪܚܐܙܐ ܡܚܐܠ ܠܐܚܕܢ *GWLU* > BCF   a e p r s^b u v
   XIV. 3*† ܡܠ (sine add.) *GWLU* > BCF   a e p r s^b u v [A hiat]
   XV. 11*† ܪܘܐܪܠܐ ܪܘܪܠܐ *GWLU* > BF   a e p r [s^b] u v z^1 [AC hiant]
   XVI. 39*† ܡܐܪܐܐ *GWLU* > BF   a e p r s^b u v z^1 [AC hiant]
   XVIII. 7*† ܦܠܙܪܐܪܠ ܐܘܪ ,ܕܘܪܐ *GWLU* > ABCF   a e p r s^b u v z^1
   „ 10*† ,ܡܠܘܙܐ *GWLU* > ABCF   a e p r s^b u v [z^1 hiat]

XXIX. 9*† ܣܘܡ [ܪܚܘܡܪܝܐ] G W L U > ABF   a c p
    r sᵇ u v z¹   [C hiat]
II. VI. 20*† ܣܙܝܐ (sine add.) G W L U > ABCF   c p r sᶜʳ
    u v z¹
  „ 36*† [ܣܐܘܝ] ܝܕ G W L U > ABC[F]   e [l] p r sᵇ
    u v z¹
VIII. 14*† ܣܐܘܪܝܐ G W L U > ABCF   c l p r sᵇ u v z¹
IX. 12*† ܘܝܕ ܪܝܝܐ G W L U > ABCF   c l p r sᵇ u v z¹
XV. 18*† ܘܝܪܝܐ ܪܝܪܝܐܘܐ G W L U > BCF   c l p r sᶜʳ u v
    [A hiat]
XXVI. 21*† ܪܚܘܝܪܝܕ G W L U > ABCF   c l p r sᵇ u v z¹
XXX. 9*† [ܣܝܪܝܐ] ܝܕܐ G W L U > ABF   c p r sᵇ u v
    [C hiat]
XXXII. 25*† ܪܝܘܝܪܝܐ [ܪܝܘܐ] G W L U > ABF   a c p
    r sᵇ u v z   [C hiat]
XXXIII. 2*† ܝܣܐܪܝܐ G W L U > ABF   c p r sᵇ u v   [C hiat]

The above lists shew that the two editions L and U follow z
(or z²) even in places in which we have most right to expect that
other and better authorities would be followed. Thus in thirty-
nine places (marked above with *) $L = z$ (or z²) against the
combined authority of Lee's own three MSS., B p u *i.e.* the
Buchanan Bible and the two Oxford codices. Again in thirty-
six instances (marked above with †) U agrees with z (or z²)
though the only Nestorian MS. of Chronicles known to us
("Sachau 90") disagrees with z (or z²). Thus L and U have
brought hardly any improvements into the text of Chronicles,
but on the contrary have preserved many of the least trustworthy readings of G.

It may be added that this blind following of z (or z²) on the
part of L and U (particularly the former) is not confined to
Chronicles. The following instances are taken from the
Prophets :—

Isaiah XIII. 22. ܣܢܪܗ GL = z ("alii legūt ܣܢܪܝܘܗ" mg)

ܣܢܪ̈ܝܗ U = [ABDF] S [k] p u [C hiat]

XVI. 1. ܐܡܪ GLU = z

(ܡܪܘ) ܡܪ ABCDFS k p u

XXI. 9. ܡܢ ܟܠܗ ܣܪ̈ܝ GLU = z^{2}

Om. ܟܠܗ ABCDFS k p u z^{1}

Jer. VI. 1. ܒܢܝܡ [ܒܝܬ] GL = z

ܒܢܝܡ U = ABCFS k p u

VI. 6. ܟܘܠܗ GL = z

ܒܟܘܠܗ̇ U = ABCFS k p u

XVII. 1. ܕܡܕܒܚܝܗܘܢ (sine add.) GLU = z

Add. ܟܡܐ ܕܡܬܕܟܪܝܢ ܒܠܒܗܘܢ

ܡܕܒ̈ܚܝܗܘܢ ABCFS k p u

XVIII. 23. [ܒܗܘܢ] ܥܒܕ GLU = $z^{2\ ut\ vid}$

ܥܒܶܕ ABCFS k p u $z^{1\ ut\ vid}$

Ezek. VI. 14[1]. ܘܐܥܒܕܝܗ ܠܐܪܥܐ ܗܕܐ ܚܪܒܬܐ

ܬܕܡܪ ܡܢ ܐܪܥܐ ܕܕܒܠܬ GL = z^{2}

ܘܐܚܪܒܝܗ ܠܐܪܥܐ ܠܫܚܠܐ ܘܠܬܡܗܐ

ܡܢ ܡܕܒܪܐ ܕܕܒܠܬ U = ABCEFS

k p u^{2} v [ܡܕܒܪ̈ܐ pro ܡܕܒܪܐ u^{1}]

XXVI. 17. ܕܝܗܒܘ ܕܚܠܬܗܘܢ ܒܟܠܗܘܢ

ܥܡܘܪ̈ܝܗ ܕܐܪܥܐ $GL[U]$ = z^{2}

ܘܐܬܬܒܪܘ ܟܠܗܘܢ ܥܡܘܪ̈ܝܗ ABC

EFS k p u v

See also Ezek. VI. 8; XVI. 12, 32, 47; XVII. 6; XVIII. 17; XX. 6 (bis), 15; XXI. 10; XXIII. 7; XXVI. 3; XXVII. 14, 33; XXIX. 6;

[1] This passage is strangely enough cited by Cornill (Ezech. pp. 140, 141) among the instances which he gives of Cod. A standing alone (or almost alone) in agreement with the Massoretic text "gegen die übrigen Recensionen" of the Peshitta.

XXXI. 16; XXXIII. 20; XXXVII. 24; XXXVIII. 16; XL. 2 cited below in the section on the Codex Ambrosianus. In each of these cases the reading which Cornill assumed to be the reading of the Peshitta is simply the reading of z (or—still worse—of z^2), while the reading of the Codex Ambrosianus is with a few insignificant exceptions that also of BCEFS k p u v.

On the other hand it is clear that z was not the only MS. used for the text of G. The Editors note in one place (not in Chronicles) that certain verses are missing "in utroque manuscripto." Indeed an inscription in MS. "Syriaques 7" of the Bibliothèque Nationale ("l") claims that this MS. was used for the production of G (cp. Zotenberg, Catalogue p. 2). Two facts however speak against this claim; l, unlike z, is *clean* and *unpointed*. Perhaps the truth is that l was at the elbow (without being in the confidence) of the Editors. Still some other MS. (not yet identified) must have been used besides z to set up the type from, at least for II. Kings, a book which is represented in z by a small fragment only. However this may be, we may say with some confidence that the bulk of the O. T. was printed in G from z, for Printers' marks untouched or half erased are to be traced in this MS. through the Pentateuch, Job, Joshua, I. Kings, Chronicles, Proverbs, I. Maccabees (II. Macc. is wanting), Ezra-Nehemiah, Isaiah, Jeremiah, Ezekiel and Daniel.

§ 2. *MSS. of the Peshitta.*

(*a*) The Codex Ambrosianus (here cited as A) has been published in facsimile by Dr Ceriani (Milan 1876-83) and therefore needs little description. It contains the following books in the order given:—The Pentateuch, Job, Joshua, Judges, I. II. Samuel, Psalms, I. II. Kings, Proverbs, Wisdom, Ecclesiastes, Canticles, Isaiah, Jeremiah (with Lamentations, the Epistle of Jeremiah, and I. II. Epistles of Baruch), Ezekiel, XII. Minor Prophets, Daniel (with Bel and the Dragon), Ruth, Susanna, Esther, Judith, Sirach, I. II. Chronicles, Apocalypse

INTRODUCTION.

of Baruch, IV. Esdras, Ezra-Nehemiah (undivided), I. II. III. IV. Maccabees, Josephus B. J. book VI.

A full palæographical description of the MS. is expected from the pen of Dr Ceriani; it is enough to say here that it is written in an Estrangela hand probably of the Sixth Century.

In spite of the unfavourable opinion of Professor Cornill, this MS. seems to be, all things considered, certainly the most valuable authority which we possess for the Peshitta text of the Old Testament. Some interesting and perhaps original readings in which it stands alone against all other authorities which I have examined are the following:—

I. Chr. XII. 8. The description of the mighty men of Gad who joined David closes (in the ordinary text) with the words, "And when they *fought against* (ܡܬܟܬܫܝܢ) a mountain they rooted it out." Cod. A alone for "fought" reads "were assembled" (ܡܬܟܢܫܝܢ) thereby giving a Midrashic turn to the verse; when these 'doctors' of Gad were assembled to discuss some mountain-like difficulty, they solved it. It is interesting that in both readings כצבאים ('like the roes') is taken as a verb (כצבאם). (Compare I. V. 12. The children of Gad were under the leadership of Joel who 'taught them the Scriptures well.' In the Targum this Joel is ריש סנהדרין.)

II. IV. 9. 'And [Solomon] made *one* great court for the priests and Levites' (usual text). According to the Hebrew 'he made the court (הצר) of the priests and the great court' (עזרה). Cod. A reads simply, 'he made the new great court.'

II. X. 4. '[Lighten somewhat] of the hard *lordship* (ܡܪܘܬܗ) [of thy father]' (usual text). Cod. A alone reads 'of the hard *discipline, chastisement* (ܡܪܕܘܬܗ) [of thy father].'

II. X. 7. 'If thou wilt speak with them *good* words, they will be to thee *good* servants and subjects all the days of thy life.' Cod. A alone (in Chronicles) omits the second "good" which may indeed be a gloss; in the parallel passage of Kings all authorities omit the word.

II. XXII. 11. Jehosheba hid Joash in the bed-chamber of *her bed* (ܡܫܟܒܗ ܕܒܩܝܛܐ). This is the reading of all MSS. of Chronicles except A, and of all MSS. including A in the parallel passage of II. Kings. In Chronicles however Cod. A reads 'in the bed-chamber *of her dwelling*' (ܡܫܟܒܗ). The reading ܡܫܟܒܗ may be a later gloss introduced to make the meaning of ܩܝܛܘܢܐ (κοιτών) clear, and, as sometimes happens, the true reading in two parallel passages may be preserved in one MS. of the less read (and less frequently transcribed) of the two parallel texts.

Cornill on Cod. A.

(*b*) It seems almost necessary in this place to consider briefly the judgment passed on Cod. A by Professor Cornill (Ezechiel, pp. 140–145). It will be remembered that Cornill after reckoning up 86 places in the book of Ezekiel in which he says that Cod. A agrees with the Massoretic text 'gegen die übrigen Recensionen' of the Peshitta, concludes that the text of Cod. A has been corrected and altered on a large scale to conform to the Massoretic, and that 'among all accessible texts of the Peshitta A is the worst' (Ezechiel, p. 145).

An able answer to Professor Cornill has been already given (ZATW 1889, pp. 161–210) by Dr Alfred Rahlfs, but since Rahlfs, while rightly emphasising the importance of the Urumia edition of the Peshitta for textual criticism, has not appealed directly to MSS., there is room for a second answer based on a direct appeal to MSS. After a careful examination of test passages in eight or ten MSS. (some of the highest importance) I am led to the conclusion that Professor Cornill's judgment on Cod. A cannot be maintained. Cod. A in its agreement with the Massoretic text does *not* stand alone to the extent suggested by Cornill's words. The reverse is very often the case and the printed texts *GL* (and sometimes *U* also; I omit *W* as a mere reprint of *G*) are found to rest on one or two late MSS., while the older MSS. unite to support the rival readings of Cod. A. The agreement of the Codex Ambrosianus with the Massorets is no doubt a fact, but the whole truth seems to be that *a text formed from the best and oldest MSS. would agree about as frequently as Cod. A with the Massoretic and would disagree as frequently with the present printed text.* The following instances chosen out of Professor Cornill's eighty-six will support this contention.

EZEKIEL.

VI. 8. ܡܢܟܘܢ (2do) *GLU* = z
Om. *ABCEFS k p u v

VII. 4. ܬܗܘܐ *GLU* = BCFS k v
ܢܗܘܢ *AE

15. ܒܒ̈ܬܐ *GLU* = BCS k v
ܒܒܝܬܐ *AEF

VIII. 3. ܘܬܩܡ *GLU* = BCS k
ܕܬܩܡ *AEF

5. ܕܓܪܒܝܐ (sine add.) *GL* = u v z (*not* C p)
Add. ܘܐܪܝܡܬ ܥܝ̈ܢܝ ܠܐܘܪܚܐ ܕܓܪܒܝܐ *U*
= *ABC post ras E supra ras FS k p

6. ܕܥܒܕܝܢ (2do) (sine add.) *GL* = BCS k
Add. superscr. ܥܠ ܦܘܪܫ ܚܘܠܗܘܢ AEF u
[*U* ܕܥܠ ܦܘ ܚܘ]

XII. 13. ܘܠܐ ܢܚܙܝܗ̇ ܠܐܪܥܐ ܘܐܦ ܬܡܢ ܢܡܘܬ *GL*[*U*]
= p u v z
[*U* ܘܬܡܢ sine ܐܦ]
ܘܠܐ ܢܚܙܝܗ̇ ܘܬܡܢ ܢܡܘܬ *ABCEFS k

XIII. 2. ܡܪ̈ܘܬܐ (sine add.) *GL* = B ut vid v z
Add. ܗܟܢܐ ܐܡܪ ܡܪܝܐ ܡܪ̈ܘܬܐ *U* = *A
[C om. ܡܪܝܐ] EFS k p u

* "A gegen die übrigen Recensionen [der Peschito]." CORNILL.

XVI. 12. ܘܩܕ̈ܫܐ ܕܕܗܒܐ ܒܐܕܢ̈ܝܟܝ | ܘܒܪ̈ܘܠܐ ܒܝܬ
ܚܢ̈ܝܟܝ *GL* = z
Transp. clausulas et om. ܕܕܗܒܐ *U* = *ABCE
FS k [p u v add. ܕܕܗܒܐ]

32. ܐܢܬܬܐ *GLU* = z
Om. *AB[C om. ܐܝܟ ܐܢ̄] EFS k p u v

47. ܕܒܪ ܩܠܝܠ *GL* = z
ܒܪ ܩܠܝܠ *U* = *ABCEFS k p v [ܒܪ u]

56. ܫܘܥܬ ܣܕܘܡ *GL* = p u v z
Transp. verba *U* = *ABCEF^ras^ S k

57. ܗܘ̈ܝ ܠܗ (sine add.) *GL* = u v z
Add. ܘܚܒ̈ܫܢ ܗܘ̈ܝ ܠܗ *U* = *ABCEFS k p

XVII. 6. ܘܡܫܒܚܬ *GLU* = p v z
ܡܫܒܚܬ *ABCEFS k u² [hiat u¹]
ܘܫܒܘ̈ܪܝܗ (sine add.) *G* = z
Add. ܗܘܘܢ *LU* = *ABCEFS k p u² [hiat u¹] v

XVIII. 17. ܢܣܒ (sine add.) *GL* = z
Add. ܘܬܚܪܐ ܠܐ ܢܣܒ *U* = *ABCEFS k p u v

XX. 5. ܠܗ [ܘܐܬܝܕܥܬ] *GL* = v z
ܠܗܘܢ *U* = *ABCEFS k p u

6. ܘܒܝܘܡܐ ܗܘ *GL* = z²
ܒܗ ܒܝܘܡܐ ܗܘ *U* = *ABCEFS k p u v
ܐܦܩܬ (sine add.) *GL* = z²
Add. ܠܗܘܢ *U* = *ABCEFS k p u v

15. ܥܠܝܗܘܢ *GL* = z
ܠܗܘܢ *U* = *ABCEFS k p u v

XXI. 10. [*Heb.* 15] ܡܫܠܠܐ (sine add.) *GLU* = z
Add. ܐܬܫܠܠ *ABCEFS k p v [u hiat]

* "A gegen die übrigen Recensionen [der Peschito]." Cornill.

XXIII. 7. ܟܠ ^ ܓܒ̈ܝܐ *G*=z

Ins. (ܒܟܠܗܘܢ) ܟܠܗܘܢ *LU*=*ABCEFS k p u v

21. ܘܦܩܕܬܟܝ *GL*=p u v z

ܘܦܩܕܬܝ *U*=*ABC[E ܘܦܩܕܬ]FS k

XXIV. 10. ܘܪܬܚ *GL*=vz

ܘܐܪܬܚ *U*=*ABCEFS k p u

XXVI. 3. ܥܠܝܟܝ (sine add.) *GL*=z[2] (om. per homoeoteleuton ܨܘܪ ܘܐܣܩ ܥܠܝܟܝ v z[1])

Add. ܨܘܪ *U*=*ABCEFS k p u

XXVII. 14. ܘܪ̈ܟܫܐ *GL*=z

ܪ̈ܟܫܐ *U*=*ABCEFS k p u v

26. ܐܥܠܘ *GL*=p v z

ܐܥܠܘܟܝ *U*=*ABCEFS k

33. ܕܬܐܓܘܪܬܟܝ *GL*=z

Praem. ܘ *U*=*ABCEFS k p u v

XXVIII. 19. ܘܗܘܐ *GLU*=p u v z

ܕܗܘܐ *ABCEFS k

XXIX. 6. ܕܢܕܥܘܢ *GLU*=z

ܘܢܕܥܘܢ *ABCEFS k p u v

XXX. 11. ܕܥܡܗ *GLU*=p u v z

ܕܥܡ̈ܡܐ *ABCEFS k

XXXI. 16. ܒܓܒ̈ܝܐ *GL*=z

ܘܓܒ̈ܝܐ *U*=*ABCEFS k p u v

XXXII. 27. ܢܫܟܒܘܢ *GLU*=p u z

Praem. ܠܐ *ABCEFS k v

* "A gegen die übrigen Recensionen [der Peschito]." Cornill.

XXXIII. 20. ⟨syr⟩ GL = z
⟨syr⟩ U = *ABCEFS k p u v
XXXVII. 24. ⟨syr⟩ GL = z
Add. ⟨syr⟩ U = *ABCEFS k p u v
XXXVIII. 14. ⟨syr⟩ GL = p u v z
Om. U = *ABCEFS k
16. ⟨syr⟩ GL = z
⟨syr⟩ U = *ABCEFS k p u v
XXXIX. 4. ⟨syr⟩ [⟨syr⟩] GLU = BCS k p v
⟨syr⟩ *AEF
18. ⟨syr⟩ G = u v z
⟨syr⟩ LU = *ABCEFS k p
XL. 2. ⟨syr⟩
⟨syr⟩ (tantum) GLU = z
⟨syr⟩
⟨syr⟩ *ABCE[FS][1] k p u [v][1]

The Buchanan Bible.

(c) The Buchanan Bible (Camb. Univ. Lib. Oo. 1. 1, 2) is a Pandect bound in two volumes which was brought from the Malabar Coast at the beginning of the present (nineteenth) century by Dr Claudius Buchanan. It contains the following books of the Old Testament in the order given:—Pentateuch, Job, Joshua, Judges, I. II. Samuel, Psalms, I. II. Kings (the order of books thus far being that of Cod. A), Chronicles, Proverbs, Ecclesiastes, Canticles, Sirach, Isaiah, Jeremiah (with Lamentations, I. II. Epistles of Baruch, and Epistle of Jeremiah), Ezekiel, XII. Minor Prophets, Daniel (with Bel and Dragon),

---

* "A gegen die übrigen Recensionen [der Peschito]." CORNILL.
[1] FS v are here bracketed because the last three words of the reading in support of which these MSS. are quoted have not been verified in them.

Ruth, Susanna, Esther, Judith, Ezra-Nehemiah, Wisdom, I. II. III. IV. Maccabees, Esdras, Tobit. The New Testament follows, the Apocalypse being left out and the four Minor Catholic Epistles being given in a group by themselves.

Though this MS. was brought from India, we have reason to believe that its birthplace was nearer Syria. It is written in a Jacobite serta probably of the twelfth century. (See the facsimile in the late Professor Bensly's "Fourth Book of Maccabees.") Two other important MSS. written in a very similar hand are "Crawfurd Syr. 2" from which Professor Gwynn has recently (at the beginning of 1897) published a version of the Apocalypse before unknown, and " Vatican Syr. 266" which contains the three Catholic Epistles (*not* Jude also as is stated in Mai's Catalogue) and the Epistles of S. Paul. Professor Gwynn (*Apocalypse of S. John*, Introductory Dissertation, pp. CVI-CXIX; cp. Transactions R. I. A., vol. XXX, p. 347 ff.) after careful consideration of all the phenomena of the Crawfurd MS. assigns it 'probably to the last quarter of the twelfth century' and to the district of Tur-'abdin. The same date (and perhaps the same birthplace) may be assigned to the Buchanan Bible without much fear of error.

In text Cod. B is related rather to the later than the earlier MSS. In its best moments it agrees with Cod. C, but it frequently leaves C in order to company with the run of seventeenth century MSS. A few examples will illustrate the affinities of B. (The late MSS. are given without any attempt at completeness, just as there was time to collate them or not.)

(a) *Mistakes.*

  I. XIV. 11.   ܚܘܦܐ B a c p r u' v z'
  XXIII. 4.   ܪܩܠܡ B a c r v z'

(b) *Gaps.*

  I. XIII. 11.   B a c p r u v z
  II. XXX. 2.   B c p r u v z'
  „ 14—22. B a c p r u v z'
  XXXII. 17.   B a c p r u v z

(c) *Other readings.*

I. I. 46.	B a e r u v z > ACF	s^b
X. 3.	B a e p r u z > ACF	s^b
XIX. 13.	B a e p r u z > ACF	s^b
II. IV. 5.	B e p r u z > AF	s^b
V. 2.	B e p r u z > AF	s^b
VI. 32.	B e p r u v z > ACF	s^b
VII. 14.	B e p r u v [z] > AC[F]	s^b
XXIII. 11.	B e p [u] z > ACF	s^{cer}
XXIV. 7.	B e p u z > ACF	$[s^{cer}]$
XXVIII. 16.	B p u v z > ACF	s^b

Codex C.

(d) The MS. here cited as C (Brit. Mus. Add. 17104) is no. XXV. of Wright's Catalogue. The writing is Estrangela of the sixth century. It contains the book of Chronicles only and that with large gaps. From the First Book two passages are missing, viz. XIV. 12–XVII. 27 and XXII. 8 to the end of the Book. From the Second Book four passages, viz. I. 1–V. 14, XVIII. 19–29, XX. 24–32, XXIX. 5 to the end of the Book.

Though Cod. C and Cod. A belong probably to the same century they exhibit different types of text, which are preserved in later MSS., the C-type in Cod. B, the A-type—in part at least—in Cod. F. The following instances will suffice to illustrate this. The more interesting are marked with an asterisk.

I. IV. 15*.	BC [+ s^b] > AF
X. 2*.	BC [+ s^b] > AF
XI. 11 (bis)*.	BC [+ s^{cer}] > AF
„ 15*.	BC > AF
„ 23.	BC > AF [+ s^{cer}]
XII. 1.	BC [+ s^{cer}] > AF
„ 14.	BC > AF [+ s^b]
XVIII. 15*.	BC > AF [+ s^{cer}]
XIX. 13*.	BC > AF [+ s^{cer}]
II. IX. 6.	BC [+ s^b] > AF
XXII. 1*.	BC > AF

Codex Florentinus.

(*c*) Cod. F (Laurent. Orient. 58) is the Palatino-Mediceus I. of Asseman's Catalogue. It is written on parchment in a small cursive hand probably of the ninth century. As to spelling it may be noticed that prosthetic Alaph is common, we have e.g. such forms as ܐܦܠܘ — ܐܝܕܐ — ܐܕܒܐ — ܐܘܝܢ — ܐܝܪܒܐ. The full spelling of ܟܠ is rare, but I have noticed at least one instance. The form ܕܐܚܪܢܐ is common; and ܡܠܘܢ is found in one place (I. Chr. IX. 1) for ܡܢܐ. Two large portions of Chronicles (I. XII. 11–XX. 3 and II. XI. 3–XXI. 1) are given in facsimile from this MS. in Dr Ceriani's facsimile edition of the Codex Ambrosianus (Milan 1876-1883).

Asseman's account of the contents of Cod. F is inaccurate. The MS. is defective at the beginning and at the end, and contains the following books in the order given:—Leviticus (beginning XV. 13 ܐܕܘܡܐ), Numbers, Deuteronomy (wants III. 3 ܕܬܚܘܒܝ—IX. 19 ܐܬܪܟܐ), Joshua, Judges (ends at XX. 33), I. II. Samuel (beginning I. Sam. II. 18 ܚܕܐ ܕܒܥܐ), I. II. Kings (undivided), I. II. Chronicles (undivided), Psalms, Canticles from the Old and New Testaments and some extra-canonical source, the "True and Orthodox Confession of the Three Hundred and Eighteen Holy Fathers," Isaiah, Jeremiah (with Lamentations), Ezekiel, Hosea (ends at XIV. 6 ܐܡܪܐ).

A later scribe seems to have imitated the original hand. To him are due (*a*) Gen. I. 1—XXXIV. 15 written on paper and prefixed to the volume, and (*b*) a supplement at the end (also on paper) containing the missing part of the XII. Minor Prophets, Daniel (with apocryphal additions), Esther (ends IX. 18), Judith (beginning VI. 18), and Ezra (the canonical book, unfinished). I have referred to the work of this later scribe as F².

The following passages may be cited as containing interesting readings attested practically by F alone (since d l m are clearly derived from F). [Compare also I. Chron. chaps. XVIII. and XIX. passim.]

I. v. 2.	F > ABC s^b
II. vi. 36.	F > ABC s^b
XVI. 12.	F > BC s^b
XVIII. 12.	F > BC s^{cer}
„ 33.	F > BC s^{cer}
XXII. 3.	F > ABC s^{cer}
XXIII. 19.	F > ABC s^b
XXXII. 27.	F > AB s^b

The text of Cod. F is peculiar. While resembling that of Cod. A in many striking instances, it frequently departs from A (*and from all other MSS. which I have examined*) in other instances equally striking to agree with the Massoretic text. It is difficult to quell the suspicion that F would be found guilty if tried on the count brought by Professor Cornill against A. It seems quite probable that in Chronicles at least its text has been so freely conformed to the Massoretic, that its value as a witness to the text of the Peshitta is seriously lessened. Yet where A is silent through loss of text, F should surely be heard, for it seems sometimes to preserve the reading of the lost mutual ancestor of A and F. One instance of this is probably to be found in II. XIII. 5, and another in II. XXIX. 22, 23.

Codex " Sachau 90."

(*f*) MS. "Sachau 90" (s) is written on paper in a Nestorian hand with many Nestorian vowels. It has many differences of spelling from the late West Syrian MSS., e.g. the scribe writes ܠܝܫܘ and ܪܘܚܐ. It was finished according to the colophon A. Gr. 1966. i.e. A.D. 1654 or 1655. Its contents are as follows in the order given:—I. II. III. Maccabees, Chronicles, Ezra-Nehemiah, the Great Wisdom, Judith, Esther, Susanna, the Epistle of Jeremiah and the two Epistles of Baruch. Chronicles is divided into thirty-seven sections: II. Chr. I. 1 occurs in the middle of Section Eighteen.

In text Cod. s stands far above the West Syrian MSS. of the seventeenth (or sixteenth) century; indeed it must be reckoned as a primary MS, and as sometimes speaking the decisive word when the other primary MSS. viz. ABCF disagree. It contains several readings (probably original) which occur elsewhere in Cod. A only; see II. VI. 18; XIII. 4; XXIII. 3; XXIV. 1; XXVI. 16; XXVIII. 21. Cod. s supplies also some striking instances of agreement with F against most authorities; see II. XIII. 5; XXVI. 20; and XXIX. 23, places in which F perhaps preserves the reading of the lost mutual ancestor of A and F.

§ 3. *Aim and arrangement of this book.*

My object in these pages is not to give a complete apparatus criticus to Chronicles, but rather to use Chronicles to illustrate the relation of some of the chief MSS. of the Peshitta to one another and to the printed text. A critical edition of the Old Testament in the Peshitta version is badly needed, and my hope is that, if interest be aroused, the want will be supplied. In the mean time the following considerations may be of service in the use of existing helps to the textual criticism of the Peshitta. (Compare Rahlfs, ZATW 1889, pp. 165, 6.)

(1) *GLU* when they agree *may* or *may not* be independent witnesses. The reading which all three support is sometimes dependent on the single attestation of z.

(2) Only the *variations* of *L* from *G*, and of *U* from *GL* may be safely treated as significant.

(3) The variation of *L* from *G* may signify that B p u combine against z, or (in the Prophets) that BC p u combine against z.

(4) The variation of *U* from *GL* signifies as a rule that *U* has a genuine Nestorian reading; if *U* be supported in the variation by Cod. A, the reading is probably original, if *U* be supported not only by Cod. A but also by Thorndike's MSS. (Walton's Polyglot, vol. VI.), the reading is probably that of practically all the MSS.

In citing MSS. I have striven after accuracy with all my power; every reading of a primary MS. has been twice examined[1]. The readings marked "s^{cer}" have been thrice examined, twice by Dr Ceriani, and once by myself to make sure that I had made no error in transcribing the notes which Dr Ceriani most generously lent me. No reading of any MS. is cited which I have not examined with my own eyes, save with the following exceptions. Professor Guidi of Rome, though I was a stranger, sent me collations of codices d m r v for the first six chapters of I. Chronicles. Professor Sachau of Berlin very kindly collated Cod. s ("Sachau 90") in II. II. 14, XV. 17, and XVI. 12; these readings will be found in the Addenda. In one or two places (hardly more) I have quoted the Bodleian MS. Poc. 391 as "pth" from Thorndike's collation; otherwise I have never used Thorndike without verification. I have been much helped by the work done for the London Polyglot, but I have found several blemishes in it.

I have used capitals to designate MSS. which are at least as early as the thirteenth century, and small letters for the later MSS. In the case of one MS. ("r") this rule has perhaps been broken; see r in the list of MSS.

In cases in which a MS. supports a given reading but with some small variation (specially in spelling) of its own, the letter designating the MS. is as a rule silently enclosed in square brackets. If however the variation is of interest it is added within the square brackets.

In cases in which it is at all probable that a parallel passage has exercised a disturbing influence on the text, reference is made immediately to such a passage within curved brackets. In no case however has it been assumed without examination that the printed text of any parallel passage is trustworthy. References to Genesis have been verified by comparing L with Codd. AB and with Cod. D (B. M. Add. 14425, dated A.D. 464).

---

[1] Cod. S (Sachau 201) may be an exception; for I have no note of my revision of the readings of this MS.

INTRODUCTION.　xxxiii

References to Samuel and Kings rest on an examination of Codd. ABF and also of Cod. N (Camb. Univ. Add. 1964, Nestorian, XIII. century). References to Isaiah have been verified by the use of Codd. ABF and also of Cod. C (Camb. Univ. Ll. 2. 4, the "Cant." of Thorndike, dated at Edessa A.D. 1173). In any case in which the text of the parallel passage is uncertain, the authorities on both sides are given, e.g. under I. Chr. XVIII. 10 it is noted that in II. Sam. VIII. 10 ܩܡܝܫܐ is read by AF and ܩܡܝܫܐ by BN.

In order to help the reader to readily identify the words affected by a divergence of reading I have often added within square brackets from the immediate context one or more words which are unaffected by the divergence.

LIST OF MSS. CITED.

A, the Codex Ambrosianus of Milan (VI. century). It is cited mainly from the facsimile edition of Dr Ceriani (1876-1883). An asterisk marks readings taken from the MS. itself.

B, the Buchanan Bible (XII. century), Camb. Univ. Oo. 1. 1, 2.

C (of Chronicles), Brit. Mus. Add. 17104 (VI. century).

C (of the Prophets), Camb. Univ. Ll. 2. 4 (Edessa, A.D. 1173).

D (of the Pentateuch), Brit. Mus. Add. 14425 (A.D. 464).

D (of Isaiah), Brit. Mus. Add. 14432 (VI. century).

E (of Ezekiel), Brit. Mus. Add. 17107 (A.D. 541).

F, the Codex Florentinus (IX. century), Palatino-Mediceus I. of Asseman's Catalogue, now "Laurent. Orient. 58."

N (of ܟܬܒܐ ܚܕܬܐ), Camb. Univ. Add. 1964 (XIII. century). Nestorian.

S, Sachau 201 (X. century?) of Berlin. Nestorian in Estrangela character.

---

a, Codex Ambrosianus alter (A.D. 1615). West Syrian.

d, Vat. Syr. 8
l, Bib. Nat. Syr. 7 } apparently transcripts of F, supplemented from other sources where F fails.
m, Vat. Syr. 7

e, Brit. Mus. Egerton 704 (XVII. century). West Syrian.
k (for the Prophets), Camb. Univ. Add. 1965 (XVII. century). Nestorian.
p, Bodleian Poc. 391 (A.D. 1614). West Syrian.
r, Vat. Syr. 259. West Syrian.

The date of the writing of this MS. is uncertain. It was in existence A. Gr. 1800 (= A.D. 1488), for it contains a record that it changed hands in that year. At the end of Judges is the date ܐܘܢ ܐܠܦܐ ܫܬܐ, i.e. A.D. 1066, 7, and at the end of Chronicles the date ܐܘܢ ܐܠܦܐ ܙ, i.e. A.D. 1067, 8. But have these dates been *copied* from the exemplar from which r itself was copied? Cod. r is written in a cursive hand which does not seem to be as early as the eleventh century.

s, Berlin Kön. Bibl. Sachau 90 (A.D. 1654, 5). Nestorian.

s^{cer}, the readings collated by Dr Ceriani of Milan;

s^b, the readings collated by myself.

u, Bodleian 141 (A.D. 1627), Usher's MS. West Syrian.

I am compelled to think that Rahlfs has somewhat overestimated the value of u (ZATW 1889, pp. 192–199). Have we not a much older representative of the same recension in B if not also in r?

v, Vat. Syr. 258 (XVII. century?). West Syrian.

z, Bibl. Nat. Syr. 6 (XVII. century?). West Syrian, subsequently tampered with.

ERRATUM

Introduction, p. xxxiv l. 2

For	*Read*
(xvii century)	(A.G. 1804 = A.D. 1493)

I. II. CHRONICLES.

Insc. ܣܦܪ ܕܒܪܝܡܝܢ A

ܬܘܒ ܣܦܪ ܕܡܠܝ ܝܘ̈ܡܬܐ ܕܡ̈ܠܟܐ ܕܝܗܘܕܐ ܕܡܬܩܪܐ ܣܦܪ ܕܒܪܝܡܝܢ B[C om. ܬܘܒ] epr[s^b ܕܒܪ loco ܬܘܒ] u z

ܣܦܪ ܕܡܠܝ ܝܘ̈ܡܬܐ ܕܡ̈ܠܟܐ ܕܐܝܣܪܐܝܠ F (in marg. char. Estrang. ܣܦܪ ܕܒܪܝܡܝܢ; item in char. simpl. ܣܦܪ ܕܒܪܝܡܝܢ ܡܬܩܪܐ ܠܝܘܢܝܐ ܦܘܠܘܣ : ܕܡܬܩܪܐ ܒܠܫܢܐ ܕܣܘܪ̈ܝܝܬܐ)

I Chronicles I.

7. ܘܕܘܕܢܝܢ (ut Gen. 10. 4, z^2) *GWL* = z^2
ܘܕܘܪܢܝܢ (ut Gen. 10. 4, ABD) *U* = BCF d e m p r s^b u v [ܘܕܘܢܪܝܢ A]
𝔏 ורודנים (Gen. ודודנים), 𝔊 καὶ Ῥόδιοι (Gen. Ῥόδιοι).

12. ܘܩܦܐܕ̈ܘܩܝܐ *GWL* = [d m r u v ܘܩܦܘܕ̈ܘܩܝܐ ut Gen. 10. 14, F²] z
ܘܩܦܘܪ̈ܩܝܐ (ut Gen. 10. 14, ABD z) *U* = ABCF a s^b
𝔏 ואת כפתורים, 𝔗 וית קפוטקאי

17. ܘܐܫܘܕ *GWLU* = AB r v z [C legi neq.]
ܘܐܫܘܪ (ut Gen. 10. 22, ABDF² z) d m s^b (N.B. אשור apud Syros plerumque ܐܬܘܪ evenit)

[34. ܡܠܝܼܐܸ[ܐ]ܘ (ܚܒܝܫ) ܗܡܐ GWLU = ABCF a d r s^b
v z 𝔥 (𝔊^B Ἰακὼβ καὶ Ἠσαύ.)]

43. ܗܠܝ GWLU = B r v z
ܘܗܠܝ ACF d m s^b 𝔥 𝔊

46. ܠܥܣܘܪܐ GWLU = B a c r u v z
ܠܚܕܬܘܢܝ (ut Gen. 36. 35, A[B]D z) ACF
d l m s^b 𝔥 𝔊

CHAPTER II.

6. ܘܢܝܪܕ (ut 3 Reg. 5. 11, ABN et 𝔥) GWLU =
ABCF$^{ut\ vid}$ a r s^b z
ܘܢܝܪܕ v 𝔥 (= 𝔊) וִרְדַע

18. ܙܗܝ GWL = ABCF d m r s^b v z
ܙܗܝܪ (per errorem) U

34. ܡܥ ܚܣܝܐ GWLU = BCF a r s^b v z
ܡܥ ܚܣܝܐ A 𝔥 (מצרי) 𝔊

44, 46. ܗܚܕܘܐ . ܪܡܥܝ ܠܕܘܐ GWLU = BC a r s^b u v z
ܗܚܕܘܐ „ „ F [ܗܚܕܘܐ d] l
ܡܥ ܚܕܘܐ „ „ A (nulla interpunct.)
𝔥 וְעֵיפָה, 𝔊^B καὶ Γαιφαήλ, 𝔊^A καὶ Γαιφά.

CHAPTER III.

2. ܕܠܬܗ ܗܝܕ GWL = z [B legi ncq.] 𝔥
ܕܠܘܬܗ ܗܝܕ (ut 2 Sam. 3. 3, ABFN) U =
[A]CF a d e m r [s^b ܠܡܓܕܠܘܬܗ] v 𝔊
(𝔥 תלמי, 𝔊^B Θοαμαί, 𝔊^A Θολμεί.)

3. ܐܬܘܪܥܡ *GWLU* = B a [r] v z
ܐܬܪܥܡ (ut 2 Sam. 3. 5, ABFN) [A ܬܪܥܡ]
CF d m s^b ℌ 𝔊
(ℌ יִתְרְעָם, $𝔊^B$ 'Ιθαράμ, $𝔊^A$ 'Ιεθράμ)

Chapter IV.

9. ܡܝܩܪ ܥܠ ܐܚܘܗܝ, ܘܥܠ ܐܡܗ *GWLU* = z^2 (z^1 om.
ܡܝܩܪ)
ܪܫܝܡ ܥܠ ܐܚܘܗܝ, ܘܥܠ ܐܡܗ B[F] a [d] e
[l m] p r s^{cer} u v [F d l m ܐܪܫܝܡ]
ܪܫܝܡ ܥܠ ܐܡܗ ܘܥܠ ܐܚܘܗܝ, AC
ℌ נִכְבָּד מֵאֶחָיו, 𝔊 ἔνδοξος ὑπὲρ τοὺς ἀδελ-
φοὺς αὐτοῦ.
יקיר וחכים באוריתא יתיר מן אחוהי 𝔗

15. ܗܠܝܢ ܗܘܘ ܒܢܝܐ ܕܟܠܒ ܒܪ ܝܘܦܢܐ. ܘܒܢܘܗܝ ܕܟܠܒ.
GWLU = B[C] a r v z
ܗܠܝܢ ܗܘܘ ܒܢ̈ܘܗܝ ܕܦܠܘ. ܘܒܢܘܗܝ ܕܟܠܒ ܒܪ
ܝܘܦܢܐ A*F d m [s^b ܕܟܠܒ loco ܕܦܠܘ]
ℌ (=𝔊) וּבְנֵי כָּלֵב בֶּן יְפֻנֶּה (tantum)

19. ܐܘܪܝܐ *GWLU* = BC a r v z
ܗܘܪܝܐ A [F d s^b ܗܘܕܝܐ]
ℌ הוֹדִיָּה, $𝔊^A$ 'Ιουδαίας.

24. ܕܝܗܘܕܐ (sine add.) *GWLU* = d m z
Add. ܐܚܘܗܝ, ܕܫܘܡ ܐܒܘܗܝ, ܕܡܫܠܡܝܐ. ܘܟܕ
ܥܠܐ ܒܪܗ ܕܝܗܘܕܐ ABC[F] a c p r s^b u v
[Abhorret 𝔖 h. l. ab ℌ 𝔊]

38. ܘܠܒܝܬ *GWLU* = B a r v z
ܘܒܒܝܬ ACF d m s^b

4   I CHRONICLES.

41. ܠܓܘܒܐ $GWLU = $ A*CF [a e p ܠܒܓܐ] d m s^b z^2
     ܠܓܒܐ B r u v z^1 [vac. $\mathfrak{H}$ $\mathfrak{G}$]
42. ܚܕܡ ܥܡ $GWLU = $ B a r v z
     ܚܕܡ ܥܡ ACF d m s^b $\mathfrak{H}$ $\mathfrak{G}$

Chapter V.

1. ܐܒܘܟܪ ܪܐܒܠ (Gen. 49. 4 ܠܐܪܙ ABD z)
     $GWLU = $ z^2
     ܘܐܒܘܟܪ ܢܪܚܐ ABCF a d e l m p r s^b u v
     [prorsus om. z^1]
2. ܢܓܘܡ $GWLU = $ ABC a e p r s^b u v z
     ܢܓܡ F l m   [longe distat $\mathfrak{S}$ ab $\mathfrak{H}$ $\mathfrak{G}$]
11. ܘܡܥܠܬܐ ܕܐܒܢܐ $GWLU = $ BC r s^b v z
     ܕܡܠܬܐ (tantum) AF d l m   [סלכה $\mathfrak{H}$]
23. ܕܣܢܝܪ (sine add.) $GWLU = $ BF a l m p r u v z
     Add. ܘܚܪܒܐ ܠܛܘܪܐ ܕܐܪܝ ܘܛܘܪܐ ܕܣܢܝܪ ܘ
     AC s^b
     $\mathfrak{H}$ (= $\mathfrak{G}$) ושניר והר חרמון

Chapter VI.

32. ܡܕܡ ܕܚܙܪܐ $GWLU = $ BC r s^b v z
     ܡܕܡ ܕܚܙܒܐ AF d m $\mathfrak{H}$ $\mathfrak{G}$
49. ܠܚ ܕܒܚܣܐ ܚܡܙܒܝܡ ܟܠܢܗ $GWLU = $ z
     ܠܚ ܕܒܚܣܐ ܕܚܡܙܒܝܡ ܕܟܠܢܗ ABCF d e m
     p r s^b u v $\mathfrak{H}$ $\mathfrak{G}$
55. ܠܗܘܢ ܚܒܪܘܢ $GWLU = $ z^2
     ܠܗܘܢ ܚܣܒܪܘܢ ABCF a d e m p r s^b u v z^1
     $\mathfrak{H}$ להם את חברון

Chapter VII.

14. ܐܪܡܝܐ GIVLU = B z
ܐܪܡܝܐ ACF 1 s^b   [𝔐 הארמיה]

Chapter IX.

1. ܝܫܒ̈ܐ GIVLU = BC e s^b z
ܢܚܬܐ AF (ܢܚܬܐ) [longe distat 𝔖 ab 𝔐 𝔊]
ܗܘܐ ܕܐܠܗܐ GIVLU = ABC e 1 s^b u
ܥܡܗ ܕܐܠܗܐ F d

Chapter X.

2. ܠܐܒܢܪ GIVL = a e p r u z
ܠܐܒܢܕܒ U = ABCF d 1 s^b
ܘܡܝܬܘ (ut I Sam. 31. 2, ABFN*) GIVLU = BC a p r s^b u z
ܘܡܝܬܘ (ut I Sam. 31. 2, N¹) AF d 1
𝔐 (fere ac 𝔊) אבינדב

3. ܫܝܢ (sine add.) GIVLU = B a e p r u z
Add. ܐܪܟ ACF d 1 s^b [𝔐 𝔊 vac.]

7. ܐܚܘܗܝ ܓܒ GIVLU = BCF a r s^b z 𝔐 𝔊
Om. ܓܒ (ut I Sam. 31. 7, ABFN) A
ܘܒܢܘܗܝ GIVLU = BCF a r s^{cer} u z
ܘܚܬܢܘ (ut I Sam. 31. 7, ABFN) A

Chapter XI.

2. ܐܝܣܪܝܠ ܘܡܥܠܢܐ GIVL = B r u z
ܐܝܣܪܝܠ ܘܡܥܠܢܐ U = ACF s^{cer} [ܘܐܝܣܪܝܠ U]

3. ܟܠܗܘܢ ܣܒ̈ܐ ܕܒ̈ܢܝ ܐܝܣܪܐܝܠ *GWLU*=z² 𝕳 𝕲
ܟܠܗܘܢ ܫܒ̈ܛܐ ܕܐܝܣܪܐܝܠ BC a e p s^cer u
ܟܠܗܘܢ ܒ̈ܢܝܐ ܕܐܝܣܪܐܝܠ F
[A prorsus om.]

6. ܠܘܩܕܡ ܒܝܒܘܣܝܐ *GWLU*=BC a s^cer z 𝕳 𝕲
ܠܝܒܘܣܝܐ (absque ܠܘܩܕܡ) A[F ܟܠ ܟܠ ܡܢ
ܕܩܛܠ ܒܝܒܘܣܝܐ]
[2 Sam. 5. 8 ܠܝܒܘܣܝܐ tantum ABFN]

8. ܡܢ ܚܘܪܬܐ ܕܠܒܪ *GWLU*=B z
ܘܠܒܪ „ „ [A ܚܘܪܬܐ] CF s^b

11. ܕܕܘܝܕ. ܝܬܒ (ܡܬܒ) ܒܡܬܒܐ ܡܕܒܪܢܐ· ܪܫܐ (N.B. punct.) *GWLU* = BC[F ܒܡܬܒܐ] a u z
ܕܕܘܝܕ ܕܝܬܒ ܒܡܬܒܐ ܡܕܒܪܢܐ. ܪܫܐ A
[s^cer punct. post ܕܕܘܝܕ]

ܟܕܝܘ (ut 2 Sam. 23. 8, ABFN) *GWLU*=BC a s^cer z
ܟܢܝܘ AF
𝕳 (Chron. = 𝕲) vac., 𝕳 (2 Sam. 23. 8, fere ac 𝕲) עדינו

ܬܠܬ ܡܐܐ *GWLU* = BC a s^cer u z 𝕳 𝕲
ܬܡܢܡܐܐ (cf. 2 Sam. 23. 8) A[F d ܥܒܕ ܪܘܡܚܗ ܥܠ ܬܡܢܡ̈ܐܐ ܩܛܝܠܝܢ ܒܙܒܢܐ ܚܕܐ
excepto ܬܡܢܡ̈ܐܐ omnino ut 𝕳]

15. ܕܥܕܠܡ (ut 2 Sam. 23. 13, ABFN) *GWLU*=s^cer z (supra ras.) [𝕳 (=𝕲) עדלם]
ܕܥܕܪܬܡ BC a u
ܕܥܕܠܬܡ AF d l

17. ܕܐܫܬܝܬ *GWLU*=z^2 ut vid
ܐܫܬܝܬ A*BCF a e p r s^b u v z^1 ut vid

18. ܠܓܘܒܐ ܪܒܐ *GWLU*=BCF a s^cer z

Om. ܪܒܐ A ℌ 𝔊

20. ܐܒܫܝܐ *GWLU*=ABC

ܫܡܐ ܝܬܝܪܐ F d

ℌ שם (tantum)

21. ܥܠ ܬܠܬܝܢ ܡܝܩܪ ܗܘܐ *GWLU*=z

ܥܠ ܬܠܬܝܢ. ܘܡܢ ܬܠܬܝܢ ܡܝܩܪ ܗܘܐ A*BCF

a s^b ℌ

23. ܗܘܬ *GWLU*=BC a p z

ܐܝܬ ܗܘܐ AF s^cer [u sine ܐܝܬ]

[2 Sam. 23. 21, ܐܝܬ ܗܘܬ ABFN]

CHAPTER XII.

1. ܡܢܩܕܡ (1mo) *GWLU*=a c r u z

Praef. ܕ ABCF s^b

ܡܥܕܪܘܗܝ, [ܕܕܘܝܕ] *GWLU*=z²

ܒܥܕܪܘܗܝ, BC a c p r s^cer u z¹

ܠܥܕ̈ܪܘܗܝ, AF

8. ܘܣܕ̈ܪܐ [ܣܦ̈ܩܐ] *GWLU*=BCF a s^cer u z

ܘܟܐܪܣܐ A

ܘܡܠܟܐ ܕܡܬܬܟܫܝܢ *GWLU*=BCF a s^cer u z

ܘܡܠܟܐ ܕܡܬܬܟܬܒܝܢ A ℌ (וכצבאים) [Vide Introduction]

14. ܥܠ ܐܠܦ *GWLU*=BC a u z

Praem. ܚܕ AF s^b

17. ܢܦܩ ܗܘ ܠܩܕܡ Desid. apud A omn. post haec usque ad XVII. 25 (ܠܒܝܬ ܐܪܐ).

Chapter XIII (hiat A).

1. ܪܘܪܒܐ *GWL* = a z

ܪܘܪ̈ܒܢܐ *U* = BCF s^b u

ܘܫܠܝ̈ܛܢܐ *GWLU* = F a s^b u z [Praem. CF s^b ܘܡܕ̈ܒܪܢܐ]

ܘܫܠ̈ܝܛܐ BC

6. ܫܡܗ ܥܠܗܘܢ *GWLU* = z

ܫܡܗ ܥܠܘܗܝ BCF a e p r s^cer u v [vac. 𝔋 𝔊]

7. ܘܣܡܘܗ *GWLU* = u z^2 𝔋 𝔊

ܘܣܡ BCF a e p r v z^1

ܠܥܓܠܬܐ *GWLU* = z^2

ܒܥܓܠܬܐ BCF a e p r s^b u v [z^1 prorsus om.]

8. ܘܢ̈ܒܠܐ [*GW*]*LU* = B [*GW* = C ܘܢ̈ܒܠܐ]

ܘܢ̈ܒܠܝܐ F [om. s^b ܢ̈ܒܠܐ]

ܘܟܢ̈ܪܐ *GWLU* = B s^b z

ܘܒܟܢ̈ܪܐ CF

11. ܘܐܬܩܪܝܬ .. ܕܒܢܐ *GWLU* = [C][F] [s^b] z^2

Om. B a e p r u v z^1

ܘܐܬܩܪܝܬ ܕܘܟܬܐ *GWLU* = z^2 𝔋 𝔊

ܘܐܬܩܪܝ ܫܡܗ ܕܕܘܟܬܐ CF s^b

13. ܕܬܥܒܘܠ ܠܘܬܗ ܩܒܘܬܐ *GWLU* = z^2

ܠܡܥܠܘ ܠܘܬܗ ܠܩܒܘܬܗ ܕܡܪܝܐ CF [s^b ܩܒܘܬܗ]

ܠܡܥܠܘ ܩܒܘܬܗ ܕܡܪܝܐ (om. ܠܘܬܗ) B a e p r u v

14. ܘܒܪܟ *GWLU* = BCF e r s^b z 𝔋 𝔊

ܕܒܪܟ a p u

I CHRONICLES.

Chapter XIV. (hiat A)

3. ܠܗ (sine add.) $GWLU = z^2$
   ܠܗ ܠܝܗܘܐ BCF a e p rs^b u v   [𝔓 𝔊]
11. ܘܗܘܐ $GWLU$ = BF a z   𝔊
    ܘܗܘܐܢ C s^b 𝔓
    ܕܝܢ $GWLU$ = CF u^2 z^2 s^{cer}
    ܕܝܢ B a e p r u^2 z^1
12. ܠܒܝܬܝܪܒ܆ Desid. apud C xiv. 12—xvii. 27 (ܕܠܐ ܐܪܝܟ)

Chapter XVI. (hiant AC)

1. ܘܠܩܕܡ (sine add.) $GW = z$
   Add. ܡܪܡ ܡܚܪܡ ܕܐܝܬܘܗܝ LU = BF a e p r s^b u v [𝔓 𝔊]
   𝔓 (= 𝔊) לפני האלהים
2. ܘܠܩܕܡ (sine add.) $GWLU$ = B a p s^b u z^2 𝔓 𝔊
   Add. ܡܪܡ ܡܚܪܡ ܕܐܝܬܘܗܝ F d e
3. ܫܘܐ ܘܩܣܝܡ $GWLU$ = [B a s^b ܫܘ] z
   ܫܘ ܘܩܣܡܐ (cf. 2 Sam. 6. 19 L = ABFN) F
4. ܠܥܠ ܕܝܢ ܕܡܪܝܐ ܡܪܡ ܘܡܣܐ $GWLU = z^2$ 𝔓 𝔊
   Om. ܕܝܢ ܕܡܪܝܐ BF a r s^b z^1
10. ܘܢܫܬܒܚ ܒܫܡ $GWL[U$ ܘܢܫܬܒܚ] = z
    Ins. ܒܫܡ ܩܘܕܫܗ BF a e r s^b v 𝔓 (cf. 𝔊)
21. ܐܡܪ $GWLU$ = F s^{cer} z^2 𝔓 𝔊
    ܐܡܪܘ B a e r z^1

ܕܢܗܪܘܢܘܢ *GWLU*=z[2]

ܕܢܗܪܢܘܢ B a e r z[1]

ܕܢܗܪܘܢ ܐܢܘܢ F 𝔋 (=𝔊) לעשקם

25. ܘܕܚܝܠ (sine add.) *GW*=z

Add. ܗܘ *LU*=BF a r s[b]

30. ܬܙܘܥ (1mo) *GWLU*=B e r [p u ܬܙܘܥܘܢ] [s[b]

ܘܬܙܘܥ] 𝔊 (φοβηθήτω)

ܙܘܥܘ F 𝔋

39. ܘܟܕܘܡ *GWLU*=z[2] 𝔋 𝔊

ܘܟܪܘܢ BF a e p r s[b] u z[1]

ܪܒܐ (sine add.) *GWLU*=z

Add. ܕܐܝܬ BF a e p r s[b] u v 𝔋 (=𝔊) אשר

43. ܠܒܝܬܗ ‸ ܠܡܒܪܟܘ *GW*=z

Ins. ܘܗܦܟ ܕܘܝܕ ܠܒܝܬܗ *LU*=B[F] a e p r s[b] u v [𝔋 𝔊]

[Om. ܠܒܝܬܗ F 𝔋 𝔊]

CHAPTER XVII. (hiat C; hiat A usque ad *v.* 25)

1. ܐܡܪ *GWLU*=B e

ܘܐܡܪ F s[b] 𝔋 𝔊

2. ܘܥܒܕ (sine add.) *GWLU*=B e

Add. ܡܛܠ ܕܡܪܝܐ ܥܡܟ (ut 2 Sam. 7. 3, ABFN) F s[b] [𝔋 𝔊]

4. ܠܐ ܗܘܝܐ ܬܐܡܪ *GWLU*=B e s[b]

ܠܐ ܘܐܡܪ F 𝔋 𝔊

ܕܘܝܕ ‸ ܕܐܝܬ *GWLU*=B e

Ins. ܕܗܟܢܐ ܐܡܪ ܡܪܝܐ F [s[b] ܗܟܢܐ] 𝔋 𝔊

7\. ܡܢ ܒܬܪ *GIVLU*=B e

ܡܢ ܒܣܬܪ (ut 2 Sam. 7. 8, ABFN) F s[b]

9\. ܢܘܣܦܘܢ (sine add.) *GIVLU*=B s[b] 𝔥 𝔊

Add. ܬܘܒ F

10\. ܕܥܒܕܬܟ ܕܝܢܐ *GIVLU*=B s[b]

ܕܦܩܕܬܟ ܕܝܢܐ F [𝔥 צויתי שופטים]

12\. ܢܒܢܐ ܠܝ *GIVLU*=B 𝔥 𝔊

Om. ܠܝ F s[b]

18\. ܬܘܒ ܕܘܝܕ *GIVLU*=B 𝔥 𝔊

ܬܘܒ ܥܒܕܟ F [s[b] ܕܘܝܕ ܥܒܕܟ]

ܚܟܡ *GIVLU*=B

Praem. ܐܢܬ F s[b] 𝔥 (=𝔊) ואתה ידעת

19\. ܥܒܕܬ ܠܗ *GIVLU*=B s[b]

Om. ܠܗ F 𝔥 𝔊

21\. ܘܦܪܩܬ ܐܢܬ ܠܟ *GIVLU*=B

Om. ܠܟ F s[b] 𝔥 𝔊

ܕܐܬܥܠܬ *GIVLU*=B s[b] [𝔥 𝔊]

ܘܐܬܥܠܬ F

22\. ܘܐܬܬܩܢܬ ܠܟ *GIVLU*=B s[b]

Om. ܠܟ F 𝔥 𝔊

24\. ܫܡܟ ܠܥܠܡ *GIVLU*=B

Om. ܠܥܠܡ F s[b]

Text. breviorem h. l. exhib. 𝔥, vac. 𝔊.

25\. ܥܠܬ A rursus incipit post hiatum.

ܠܡ ܚܕ GWLU=B a e p u z [F ܢܚܕܠܡ]
A ܚܕ ܠ
ܠܡ ܚܒܢܬ s^cer [𝔥 (=𝔊) לבנות לו]
26. ܢܚܕ܃ ܕܡܠܠܗ GWLU=BF a e s^cer z [𝔥 𝔊]
ܕܡܠܠܗ܃ ܚܨܡ A

CHAPTER XVIII.

2. ܥܩܠ GWLU=[A ܥܢܡܪ] BCF z
ܕܚܡܣ s^b [ܡܒܕ a pth]
ܕܒܪܬܐ GWLU=ABC
ܡܥܝܒܪܬ F [2 Sam. 8. 2 ܡܩܕܢ܂ܡܥܝܒܪܬ ABFN]
3. ܡܥܦܠܠ GWLU=ABC s^b
F ܡܥܒܣ
6. ܥܩܠ GWLU=[A ܥܢܡܪ] BC z
ܕܡܩܣܪ (ut 2 Sam. 8. 6, ABFN) F s^b
7. ܡܥܪܢܠ GWLU=ABC s^b
ܡܥܣܪܒ (ut 2 Sam. 8. 7, ABFN) F
ܠܟܪܝܬܐܠ ܪܘܐܟ܂ ܡܚܪܐ (ut 2 Sam. 8. 8, ABFN)
GWLU=z² 𝔥 𝔊
Om. ABCF a e p r s^b u z¹
8. ܕܚܣܘܕ ܡܥܒܪܪܐ GWLU=ABC s^b
Om. F 𝔥 𝔊
10. ܡܥܒܣܘܢ܂ (2 Sam. 8. 10 AF, ܡܥܒܚܘܢ܂ BN) GWLU
=z²
ܡܥܦܠܠܘ ABCF a e p r s^b u v [z¹ prorsus om.]
𝔥 (ויכהו), 𝔊 (καὶ ἐπάταξεν αὐτόν).

ܡܪܒܘܬܐ (sine add.) *GWLU* = s[cer] z[2]

Add. ܗܘ ABCF a

15. ܡܥܒܪܢܐ (2 Sam. 8. 16 ܡܥܗܕܢܐ ABFN) *GWLU* = BC a z

ܕܡܥܗܕܪ AF s[cer] 𝔥 𝔊

Chapter XIX.

2. ܚܣܕܐ ܥܡ ܚܢܘܢ *GWLU* = A* s[cer] z[2]

,, ܥܠ ,, BC a p r u z[1]

,, ܛܝܒܘܬܐ ܥܡ (ut 2 Sam. 10. 2, ABFN) F

𝔥 חסד עם חנון, 𝔊 ἔλεος μετὰ Ἀνάν.

3. ܠܘܬܢ *GWLU* = ABC

ܠܘܬܟ (ut 2 Sam. 10. 3, ABFN) F s[b] 𝔥 𝔊

5. ܕܒܗܬܝܢ ܗܘܘ *GWLU* = B

Add. ܛܒ ACF s[b] 𝔥 (מאד) 𝔊 (σφόδρα)

ܡܛܠ ܕܗܘܘ ܓܒܪ̈ܐ ܒܗܬܝܢ ܛܒ (ut 2 Sam. 10. 5, ABFN nisi ܐܢܫ̈ܐ pro ܓܒܪ̈ܐ) F omnino ut 𝔥

6. ܘܡܢ ܐܕܘܡ *GWLU* = ABC s[cer]

Om. F 𝔥 𝔊

7. ܘܡ̈ܠܟܐ ܕܐܕܘܡ *GWLU* = ABC

Om. F

(Text. breviorem h. l. exhib. 𝔥 𝔊)

9. ܡ̈ܠܟܐ *GWLU* = ABC s[b] 𝔥 𝔊

ܬܠܬܐ ܡ̈ܠܟܝܢ F

11. ܘܣܕܪ ܠܘܩܒܠ ܒܢܝ ܥܡܘܢ *GWLU* = [B]CF s[cer] u [𝔥 𝔊]

Om. A

I CHRONICLES.

13. ܘܐܬܚܙܩ ܘܐܬܚܝܠ ܘܥܡܗ ‎ GWLU = B a e p r u z
 ܘܐܬܚܝܠܘ ܘܐܬܚܙܩ (absque ܘܥܡܗ) ACF s^b
 ܚܠ ܐܦ ܚܢܢ ‎ GWLU = BC a p r u
 Praem. ܘܐܬܟܫܪ AF s^b
 𝔥 (v. 13a) חזק ונתחזקה בעד עמנו וגו׳
 𝔊^A (v. 13a) ἀνδρίζου καὶ ἐνισχύσωμεν περὶ τοῦ λαοῦ ἡμῶν· κ.τ.λ.
 ܕܐܠܗܐ GWLU = B a
 ܕܐܠܗܐ ACF s^b 𝔥 𝔊^A (𝔊^B hiat)

16. ܐܪܡ GWLU = BCF s^{cer} 𝔥
 Om. A 𝔊
 ܘܨܘܒܐ GWLU = BF u z
 ܘܨܘܒܐ (ut 2 Sam. 10. 16, AB$^{ut\ vid}$ FN) AC s^{cer}
 𝔥 ושופך, 𝔊^A καὶ Σωφάχ.

19. ܘܐܫܠܡܘ (ut 2 Sam. 10. 19, AB[F]N) GWLU = [A]CF
 ܘܐܫܠܡ B s^{cer}

Chapter XX. (a ver. 4 hiat F)

3. ܘܒܡܓܪܐ GWLU (per errorem?)
 ܘܒܡܓܪܐ ABC[F sine sey.] a d p r s^b u z
 ܒܗܘܢ GWLU = BCF a s^{cer}
 ܒܗܘܢ A
 ܒܡܘܪܓܐ ܕܦܪܙܠܐ ... ܥܡܐ GWLU = BCF s^{cer}
 Plur. ter habet A

4. Desid. apud F xx. 4—xxv. 1 (ܘܡܚܫܒܐ)

I CHRONICLES.

4, 5. ܘܗܘ ܚܬܪ ܠܝܫܝ . ܚܒܪܗܘܢ ܘܕܡ ܡܘܪܐ ܒܪ
ܦܠܛܝܐ ܘܡܦܠ ܐܠܝܫܘܥ ܕܝ ܗܠܝܢ ܠܠܫܬ. *GWLU*
= z^2 𝔓 𝔊
    Om. ABC   a d e p r s^b u z¹

5. ܘܪܘܡܚܐ (ut 1 Sam. 17. 7, ABFN, 𝔓 להבת) *GWLU*
= ABC
    ܘܢܨܒܬܐ (ut 2 Sam. 21. 19, AB^{ut vid} FN) s^b 𝔓 𝔊

6. ܬܘܒ ܠܓܪܬܐ ܠܓܪܬܐ *GWLU* = z
    ܠܓܪܬܐ ܬܘܒ ܠܓܪܬܐ ABC [a p] s^b u
    ܠܬܫܡܫܬܐ *GWLU* = B   a d m z
    ܠܬܫܡܫܬܐ AC s^b
8. ܠܬܫܡܫܬܐ *GWLU* = B   a d m u z
    ܠܬܫܡܫܬܐ AC s^b

CHAPTER XXI. (F hiat)

1. ܘܐܩܝܡ *GWLU* = BC   a d e m s^{cer} u z
    ܘܐܩܝܡܗ A

2. ܘܐܡܪ *GWLU* = BC   a d e m s^{cer} u z   𝔓 𝔊
    ܘܐܡܪܗ A

5. ܓܒܪܐ ܣܝܦ *GWLU* = BC
    ܣܝܦ ܓܒܪܐ A   p s^{cer}

6. ܘܠܐ ܓܕ *GWLU* = BC   s^{cer}
    Add. ܗܘܐ A   [longe distat 𝔖 ab 𝔓 𝔊]

12. ܟܦܢܐ *GIV* = z
    ܟܦܢܐ *LU* = ABC   d m
    ܒܐܪܥܐ *GWLU* = BC   a z   [vac. 𝔓 𝔊]
    ܒܐܪܥܟ (ut 2 Sam. 24. 13, ABFN) A s^b

ܬܬܡܣܪ (ut 2 Sam. 24. 13, ABFN) *GWLU*=A*B
a s^b
ܕܬܬܡܣܪ C

15. ܘܐܬܒܝܐܐ *GWL*=z
ܘܐܬܒܝܐ *U*=ABC a s^b

17. ܠܡܪܝܐ (sine add.) *GWLU* = z² (ܠܥܡܐ pro ܠܡܪܝܐ z¹)
Add. ܐܢܐ ܗܘ ܕܐܡܪܬ ܕܐܡܢܐ ܠܥܡܐ (ܥܡܐ)
ABC a e p r s^b u v 𝔥 𝔊
ܚܒ̈ܝ *GW*[*U* sine sey.] = [AC u ܚܒܝܘ]
[B ܚܒܝ̈] [s^b sine sey.] r z 𝔥 𝔊
ܚܒ̈ܝ *L* (per errorem) = [a p ܚܒܝܗܘܢ]

18. ܦܩܕ ܢܒܝܐ *GWLU*=BC a d m p s^cer u
ܗܘ ܩܕܡ (ut 2 Sam. 24. 18 F, ܗܘ ܟܕ ABN) A*

21. ܥܠ ܐܪܥܐ *GWLU*=B a
ܒܐܦܘܗܝ ܠܐܪܥܐ A[C ܐܪܥܐ] s^cer
𝔥 ארצה, 𝔊 ἐπὶ τὴν γῆν.

22. ܬܬܟ݂ܠܐ *GW*=z [ad construct. verb. cf. II. xvi. 3, *L*=BCF]
ܘܬܬܟܠܐ (ut 2 Sam. 24. 21, ABF [hiat N]) *LU* =A*BC a d e m p r s^b u
𝔥 ותעצר, 𝔊 καὶ παύσεται.

CHAPTER XXII. (hiat F; a *ver.* 8 hiat C)

1. ܕܐܝܣܪ[ܐ]ܝܠ *GWLU*=BC s^cer
ܒܐܝܣܪܝܠ A [𝔥 לישראל]

5. ܗܘ ܐܡܝܪܐ *GWLU*=B a
ܗܘ ܐܡܝܪ AC s^b

8. ܡܛܠ ܕܕܡܐ Desid. apud C I. xxii. 8—II. v. 14.

12. ܐܘܪܚܐ ܕܦܘܩܕܢܟ *GWLU* = B a

ܐܘܪܚܐ ܕܦܘܩܕܢܝܢ A s^b [vac. 𝔏 𝔊]

13. ܘܐܢܗܘ ܕܬܛܪ *GWLU* = [A ܕܬܥܒܕ perp.] B e

ܐܢ ܗܘ ܕܬܛܪ (sine ܘ) s^cer 𝔏 𝔊

14. ܠܒܢܝܢܐ ܠܒܝܬܗ *GWLU* = B a e u

ܠܒܢܝܢܐ ܕܒܝܬܗ A s^b

ܦܐܪܐ (sine add.) *GWLU* = B a e u 𝔏 𝔊

Add. ܡܒܢܝܐ A [s^cer ܡܒܢ̈ܝܢܐ]

ܕܫܘܠܡܐ ܗܘ *GWLU* = B a e u

ܕܫܠܡ ܗܘ A s^b

Chapter XXIII (hiant CF).

1. ܘܣܒܥ ܒܝܘܡܬܗ *GWLU* = z

ܘܣܒܥ ܝܘ̈ܡܬܗ AB a d e m p r s^b u v

4. ܥܣܪܝܢ ܘܐܪܒܥܐ ܒܪ̈ܒܘܢ ܥܠ ܐܠܦ *GWLU* = A s^b z

ܐܠܦܝܢ (loco ܒܪ̈ܒܘܢ) B a e r z^1 [𝔏 (= 𝔊) אלף]

14. ܐܬܩܪܝ‸ ܫܒܛܐ *GWLU* = B d e m p r u z

Ins. ܡܢ A s^b

𝔏 (= 𝔊) *v.* 14 b בניו יקראו על שבט הלוי

24. ܥܠ ܒܝ̈ܬܐ ܕܒܝܬܗ *GWLU* = B e z

ܕܐܬܟܬܒܘ ܒܒܝܬܗ (loco ܕܒܝܬܗ) A s^b

Chapter XXV (hiat C).

1. ܘܪ̈ܘܪܒܢܘܗܝ: ܫܠܐ *GWLU* = B [p] u

ܘܪ̈ܘܪܒܢ ܫܠܐ A s^cer 𝔏 𝔊

30, 31. Habent hos versus *GWLU* = z^2
Om. ABF d e m r s^b z^1

Chapter XXVI.

12. ܒܝܬ ܡܘܕܝܢܐ Desid. xxvi. 13—xxvii. 34 apud *GWLU* = BF a e [d l spatio relicto] p r u v z
Add. xxvi. 13—xxvii. 34 A s^{cer} 𝔓 𝔊
Cod. A sic pergit :—

ܘܐܪܡܘܣ
ܦܣܐ ܕܒܘܪܐ ܐܝܟ ܪܒܐ.
ܠܒܝܬ ܐܒܗ̈ܝܗܘܢ. ܠܬܪܥܐ
14 ܘܬܪܥܐ. ܘܢܦܠܬ ܦܣܬܐ
ܠܡܕܢܚܐ. ܠܫܠܡܝܐ ܘܙܟܪܝܐ
ܒܪܗ. ܡܠܟܐ ܒܣܘܟܠܐ.
ܐܪܡܘܣ ܦ̈ܣܐ. ܘܢܦܩܬ
15 ܦܣܬܗ ܠܓܪܒܝܐ. ܠܥܘܒܕ ܐܕܘܡ
ܠܬܝܡܢܐ. ܘܠܒ̈ܢܘܗܝ ܒܝܬ
16 ܫ̈ܦܐ. ܠܫܘܦܝܡ ܘܠܚܘܣܝܐ.
ܠܡܥܪܒܐ. ܒܬܪܥܐ ܠܬܪܥܐ
ܕܡܬܩܪ ܒܫܒܝܠܐ ܕܣܠܩ.
ܡܛܪܬܐ ܠܘܩܒܠ ܡܛܪܬܐ
17 ܠܡܕܢܚܐ. ܠܘ̈ܝܐ ܫܬܐ
ܠܡܕܢܚܐ. ⌜ܠܘ̈ܝܬܐ⌝[1] ܐܪܒܥܐ.

[1] s^{cer} ܠܘܝܬܐ ܐܪܒܥܐ (sine seyamis)

I CHRONICLES.

---

¹ scer add.
² scer sic interpungit.

26 ܫܠܡܝܬ ܒܪܗ. ܗܘ ܫܠܡܝܬ
ܘܐܚܘܗܝ، ܥܠ ܟܘܠ
ܐܘܨܪܐ ܕܩܘܕܫܐ ܕܩܕܫ ܕܘܝܕ
ܡܠܟܐ. ܘܪ̈ܫܝ ܐܒ̈ܗܬܐ
ܘܪ̈ܘܪܒܢܐ ܕܐ̈ܠܦܐ ܘܕܡ̈ܐܘܬܐ.
27 ܘܪ̈ܘܪܒܢܐ ܕܚܝܠܐ ܡܢ ܩܪ̈ܒܐ
ܘܡܢ ܒܙܬܐ. ܩܕܫܘ ܠܚܘܠܐ
28 ܕܒܝܬܗ ܕܡܪܝܐ. ܘܟܘܠ
ܕܩܕܫ ܫܡܘܐܝܠ ܚܙܝܐ.
ܘܫܐܘܠ ܒܪ ܩܝܫ. ܘܐܒܢܝܪ
ܒܪ ܢܝܪ ܘܝܘܐܒ. ܒܪ ܨܪܘܝܐ.
ܘܟܠ ܕܡܩܕܫ ܥܠ ܐܝܕܘܗܝ،
ܕܫܠܡܝܬ ܘܕܐܚܘ̈ܗܝ.
29 [1]ܠܝܨܗܪܝܐ. ܟܢܢܝܐ ܘܒ̈ܢܘܗܝ.
ܠܥܒܝܕܬܐ ܒܪܝܬܐ ܥܠ
ܐܝܣܪܐܝܠ. ܠܫ̈ܠܝܛܢܐ ܘܠܕ̈ܝܢܐ.
30 ܠܚܒܪ̈ܘܢܝܐ. ܚܫܒܝܐ ܘܐܚ̈ܘܗܝ،
ܒ̈ܢܝ ܚܝܠܐ. ܐܠܦ ܘܫܒܥܡܐܐ[2]
ܥܠ ܡܥܒܪܐ ܕܐܝܣܪܝܠ. ܡܢ
ܥܒܪܐ ܕܝܘܪܕܢ ܘܠܡܥܪܒܐ.
ܠܟܠ ܥܒܝ̈ܕܬܐ ܕܡܪܝܐ
31 ܘܠܫܘܠܛܢܐ ܕܡܠܟܐ. ܠܚܒܪ̈ܘܢܝܐ
ܝܪܝܐ ܪܝܫܐ. ܠܚܒܪ̈ܘܢܝܐ
ܠܬܘܠܕ̈ܬܗܘܢ. ܠܒܝܬ

[1] sic [2] sic

ܐܒܗ̈ܝܗܘܢ ܒܫܢܬ ܐܪ̈ܒܥܝܢ
ܠܡܠܟܘܬܗ ܕܕܘܝܕ ܐܬܒܥܝܘ.
ܘܐܫܬܟܚܘ ܒܗܘܢ ܓܢ̈ܒܪܐ
ܚܝܠܐ. ܒܝܥܙܝܪ ܕܓܠܥܕ.
32 ܘܐܚܘ̈ܗܝ ܒܢ̈ܝ ܚܝܠܐ ܬܪܝܢ
ܐܠܦ̈ܝܢ ܘܫܒܥܡܐܐ ܪ̈ܝܫܐ
ܐܒܗ̈ܬܐ. ܘܐܫܠܛ ܐܢܘܢ
ܕܘܝܕ ܡܠܟܐ. ܥܠ ܒܢ̈ܝ ܪܐܘܒܝܠ
ܘܒܢ̈ܝ ܓܕ ܘܥܠ ܦܠܓܗ ܕܫܒܛܐ
ܕܡܢܫܐ. ܠܟܠ ܦܘܠܚܢܐ
ܕܐܠܗܐ ܘܦܘܠܚܢܐ ܕܡܠܟܐ.

Chapter XXVII.

1 ܘܒܢ̈ܝ ܐܝܣܪܝܠ ܠܡܢܝܢܗܘܢ.
ܪ̈ܝܫ ܐܒܗ̈ܬܐ ܘܪ̈ܒܢܐ
ܕܐ̈ܠܦܐ ܘܕܡܐܘܬ̈ܐ.
ܘܣܦܪ̈ܝܗܘܢ ܕܡܫܡܫܝܢ ܠܡܠܟܐ.
ܠܟܠ ܦܘܠܚܢܐ ܕܦܠܓܘܬܐ
ܕܥܐܠܐ ܘܢܦܩܐ. ܝܪܚܐ
ܒܝܪܚܐ ܠܟܠ ܝ̈ܪܚܐ ܕܫܢܬܐ
ܟܠ ܦܠܓܘܬܐ ܚܕܐ. ܥܣܪܝܢ
2 ܘܐܪܒܥܐ ܐܠܦ̈ܝܢ ܟܠ
ܦܠܓܘܬܐ ܩܕܡܝܬܐ ܠܝܪܚܐ

ܩܕܡܝܐ. ܝܫܒܥܡ ܒܪ ܙܒܕܐܝܠ
ܘܥܠ ܦܠܓܘܬܗ ܥܣܪ̈ܝܢ
3 ܘܐܪܒܥܐ ܐ̈ܠܦܝܢ ܡܢ ܒܢܘ̈ܗܝ
ܕܦܪܨ. ܪ̈ܫܢܐ ܕܟܠ ܪ̈ܘܪܒܢ
ܚ̈ܝܠܘܬܐ ܕܝܪܚܐ ܩܕܡܝܐ.
4 ܘܥܠ ܦܠܓܘܬܐ ܕܝܪܚܐ
ܬܪܝܢܐ. ܕܘܕܝ ܚܘܚܝܐ.
ܘܦܠܓܘܬܗ. ܘܡܩܠܘܬ
ܫ̈ܠܝܛܐ. ܘܥܠ ܦܠܓܘܬܗ ܥܣܪ̈ܝܢ
5 ܘܐܪܒܥܐ ܐܠܦܝܢ. ܪܒ ܚܝܠܐ
ܬܠܝܬܝܐ ܠܝܪܚܐ ܬܠܝܬܝܐ.
ܒܢܝܐ ܒܪ ܝܘܕܥ ܟܗܢܐ ܪܫܐ.
ܘܥܠ ܦܠܓܘܬܗ ܥܣܪ̈ܝܢ
6 ܘܐܪܒܥܐ ܐ̈ܠܦܝܢ. ܗ̣ܘ ܒܢܝܐ
ܓܢܒܪܐ ܕܬܠܬܝܢ. ܘܥܠ ܬܠܬܝܢ.
ܘܦܠܓܘܬܗ ܕܥܡܝܙܒܕ ܒܪܗ.
7 ܪܒܝܥܝܐ ܠܝܪܚܐ ܪܒܝܥܝܐ.
ܠܥܣܐܝܠ[1] ܐܚܘ̈ܗܝ ܕܝܘܐܒ.
ܘܙܒܕܝܐ ܒܪܗ ܡܢ ܒܬܪܗ.
ܘܥܠ ܦܠܓܘܬܗ ܥܣܪ̈ܝܢ
8 ܘܐܪܒܥܐ ܐ̈ܠܦܝܢ. ܚܡܝܫܝܐ
ܠܝܪܚܐ ܚܡܝܫܝܐ. ܪܒܐ
ܫܡܗܘܬ. ܝܙܪܚܝܐ. ܘܥܠ

---

[1] sic

ܦܠܓܘܬܗ ܥܣܪ̈ܝܢ ܘܐܪ̈ܒܥܐ
9 ܐ̈ܠܦܝܢ. ܬܫܝܥܝܐ ܠܝܪܚܐ
ܬܫܝܥܝܐ. ܥܝܪܐ ܒܪ
ܥܩܫ ܬܩܘܥܝܐ. ܘܟܠ
ܦܠܓܘܬܗ ܥܣܪܝܢ ܘܐܪ̈ܒܥܐ
10 ܐ̈ܠܦܝܢ. ܥܣܝܪܝܐ ܠܝܪܚܐ
ܥܣܝܪܝܐ. ܚܠܨ ܦܠܘܢܝܐ ܡܢ
ܒܢܘ̈ܗܝ ܕܐܦܪܝܡ. ܘܟܠ
ܦܠܓܘܬܗ ܥܣܪ̈ܝܢ ܘܐܪ̈ܒܥܐ
11 ܐ̈ܠܦܝܢ. ܚܕܥܣܪܝܐ ܠܝܪܚܐ
ܚܕܥܣܪܝܐ. ܣܒܟܝ ܚܘܫܬܝܐ
ܕܡܢ ܒܝܬ ܙܪܚ. ܘܟܠ
ܦܠܓܘܬܗ ܥܣܪܝܢ ܘܐܪ̈ܒܥܐ
12 ܐ̈ܠܦܝܢ. ܬܪܥܣܪܝܐ ܠܝܪܚܐ
ܬܪܥܣܪܝܐ. ܐܒܝܥܙܪ ܥܢܬܘܬܝܐ.
ܡܢ ܕܒܝܬ ܒܢܝܡܝܢ. ܘܟܠ
ܦܠܓܘܬܗ ܥܣܪܝܢ ܘܐܪ̈ܒܥܐ
13 ܐ̈ܠܦܝܢ. ܥܣܪܝܐ ܠܝܪܚܐ
ܥܣܪܝܐ. ܡܗܪܝ ܢܛܘܦܬܝܐ.
ܡܢ ܕܒܝܬ ܙܪܚ. ܘܟܠ
ܦܠܓܘܬܗ ܥܣܪܝܢ ܘܐܪ̈ܒܥܐ
14 ܐ̈ܠܦܝܢ. ܕܚܕܥܣܪ ܠܝܪܚܐ
ܕܚܕܥܣܪ. ܒܢܝܐ ܦܪܥܬܘܢܝܐ.
ܡܢ ܒܢܘ̈ܗܝ ܕܐܦܪܝܡ. ܘܟܠ

ܦܠܓܘܬܗ ܥܣܪܝܢ ܘܐܪ̈ܒܥܐ.
15 ܕܬܪܬܥܣܪ ܠܝܪܚܐ ܕܬܪܬܥܣܪ.
ܚܠܕܝ ܢܛܘܦܬܝܐ. ܡܢ ܕܒܝܬ
ܥܬܢܝܐܝܠ. ܘܥܠ ܦܠܓܘܬܗ
ܥܣܪܝܢ ܘܐܪ̈ܒܥܐ ܐ̈ܠܦܝܢ.
16 ܘܥܠ ܫܒܛܐ ܕܐܝܣܪܝܠ.
ܠܪܘܒܝܠܝܐ ܡܕܒܪܢܐ. ܐܠܝܥܙܪ
ܒܪ ܙܟܪܝ. ܠܫܡܥܘܢܝܐ ܫܦܛܝܐ
17 ܒܪ ܡܥܟܐ. ܠܠܘܝ ܚܫܒܝܐ ܒܪ
ܩܡܘܐܝܠ. ܠܐܗܪܘܢ
18 ܨܕܘܩ. ܠܝܗܘܕܐ ܐܠܝܗܘ.
ܡܢ ܐܚ̈ܘܗܝ ܕܕܘܝܕ.
ܠܐܝܣܟܪ ܥܡܪܝ ܒܪ
19 ܡܝܟܐܝܠ. ܠܙܒܘܠܘܢ ܫܡܥܝܐ
ܒܪ ܥܘܒܕܝܐ. ܠܢܦܬܠܝ
ܝܪܝܡܘܬ ܒܪ ܥܙܪܐܝܠ.
20 ܠܒܢ̈ܘܗܝ ܕܐܦܪܝܡ. ܗܘܫܥ
ܒܪ ܥܙܝܐ. ܠܦܠܓܘܬ ܫܒܛܐ
ܕܡܢܫܐ. ܝܘܐܝܠ ܒܪ ܦܕܝܐ.
21 ܘܠܦܠܓܘܬܐ ܕܡܢܫܐ
ܕܒܓܠܥܕ [1]ܝܕܘܒܪ ܙܟܪܝܐ.
ܠܒܢܝܡܝܢ ܝܥܣܝܐܝܠ ܒܪ ܐܒܢܝܪ.

[1] sic

22 ܠܕܢ ܥܙܪܐܝܠ ܒܪ ܝܪܘܚܡ.
ܗܠܝܢ ܪ̈ܘܪܒܢܐ ܕܫ̈ܒܛܐ
23 ܕܐܝܣܪܝܠ. ܘܠܐ ܢܣܒ ܕܘܝܕ
ܡܢܝܢܗܘܢ ܡܢ ܒܪ ܥܣܪܝܢ
ܫܢ̈ܝܢ [1]ܘܠܬܚܬ. ܡܛܠ ܕܐܡܪ
ܡܪܝܐ ܕܢܣܓܘܢܗܝ ܠܝܣܪܝܠ
ܐܝܟ ܟܘܟ̈ܒܐ ܕܫܡܝܐ.
24 ܝܘܐܒ ܒܪ ܨܪܘܝܐ ܫܪܝ[2]
ܕܢܡܢܐ ܘܠܐ ܫܠܡ. ܘܗܘܐ
[3]ܒܗܕܐ ܪܘܓܙܐ ܥܠ
ܐܝܣܪܝܠ. ܘܠܐ ܣܠܩ ܡܢܝܢܐ
ܐܝܟ [4]ܡܢܝܢܐ. ܕܕܘܝܕ
25 ܡܢܝܡ ܠܡܠܟܐ ܕܘܝܕ. ܘܥܠ
ܐܘܨ̈ܪܐ ܕܡܠܟܐ ܥܙܡܘܬ.
ܒܪ ܥܕܐܝܠ. ܘܥܠ ܐܘܨ̈ܪܐ
ܕܚܩܠܐ. ܒܩܘܪ̈ܝܐ
ܘܒܟܦܪ̈ܘܢܐ ܘܒܡܓܕ̈ܠܐ.
26 ܝܘܢܬܢ ܒܪ ܒܘܙܝܐ. ܘܥܠ
ܥܒ̈ܕܝ ܥܒ̈ܕܬܐ ܕܚܩܠܐ
ܠܦܘܠܚܢܐ ܕܐܪܥܐ. ܥܙܪܝ

[1] sic, ܘܠܬܚܬ sᵇ [2] ܫܪܝ sᵇ [3] Om. ܒܗܕܐ sᵇ
[4] Om. (.) s^cer (sic) ܡܢܝܢܐ ܕܕܒܪܝܡܝܢ
[Heb. במספר, LXX. ἐν βιβλίῳ = ܐܝܟ ܡܢܝܢܐ]

27 ܒܪ ܠܘܒܢ. ܘܥܠ ܒܪ̈ܡܐ
ܫܡܥܝܐ ܪܡܬܝܐ. ܘܥܠ
ܡܕܡ ܕܒܟܪ̈ܡܐ ܠܐܘܨܪܐ
ܕܚܡܪܐ. ܙܒܕܝ ܫܦܡܝܐ.
28 ܘܥܠ ܙܝ̈ܬܐ ܘܫܩ̈ܡܐ
ܕܒܫܦܠܬܐ. ܒܥܠܚܢܢ ܓܕܪܝܐ.
ܘܥܠ ܐܘܨܪܐ ܕܡܫܚܐ
29 ܝܘܐܫ. ܘܥܠ ܬܘܪ̈ܐ ܕܪܥܝܢ
ܒܫܪܘܢܐ ܫܪܛܝ. ܫܪܘܢܝܐ.
ܘܥܠ ܬܘܪ̈ܐ ܕܒܥܘܡܩܐ.
30 ܫܦܛ ܒܪ ܥܕܠܝ. ܘܥܠ ܓܡ̈ܠܐ.
ܐܘܒܝܠ ܐܝܫܡܥܠܝܐ. ܘܥܠ
ܐܬ̈ܢܐ. ܝܗܘܕܐ ܡܪܘܬܢܝܐ.
31 ܘܥܠ ܥ̈ܢܐ ܝܙܝܙ ܗܓܪܝܐ.
ܟܠܗܘܢ ܗܠܝܢ ܪ̈ܘܪܒܢܐ
32 ܕܩܢܝܢܐ ܕܡܠܟܐ ܕܘܝܕ. ܘܝܘܢܬܢ
ܚܒܝܒܗ ܕܕܘܝܕ ܡܠܟܐ.
ܓܒܪܐ ܗܘܐ ܡܠܘܟܐ
ܘܣܦܪܐ[1]. ܝܚܝܐܝܠ ܒܪ
ܚܟܡܘܢ. ܥܡ ܒܢ̈ܘܗܝ
33 ܕܡܠܟܐ. ܘܐܚܝܬܘܦܠ
ܡܠܟܐ ܕܡܠܟܐ. ܘܚܘܫܝ
ܐܪܟܝܐ ܪܚܡܗ ܕܡܠܟܐ.

[1] sic, ܘܣܦܪܐ s[b]

34 ܘܡܢ ܒܬܪ ܐܚܝܬܘܦܠ. ܝܗܘܝܕܥ
ܒܪ ܒܢܝܐ. ܘܐܒܝܬܪ. ܘܪܒ
ܚܝܠܐ ܕܡܠܟܐ ܝܘܐܒ.

Chapter XXVIII. (hiat C)

1. ܘܕܫܠܝܛܝܢ *GIWLU*=BF u
 ܘܕܡܫܠܛܝܢ A s^b
7. ܠܦܘܩܕܢܝ *GIWLU*=BF s^cer u 𝔓
 ܠܦܬܓܡܝ A 𝔊
9. ܕܥܒܕܝܢ ܡܪܝܐ ܐܠܗܐ *GIWLU*=B[F d m ܐܠܗܢ]
 ܕܥܒܕܢ ܡܪܝܐ ܐܠܗܢ A s^b
 ܐܘܠܝܢ *GIWLU*=A*F s^b
 ܐܘܠܝܕ B
21. ܘܗܘܢ ܡܫܠܛܝܢ *GIWLU*=BF [s^cer ܫܠܝܛܝܢ] u
 Om. ܡܫܠܛܝܢ A*

Chapter XXIX. (hiat C)

1. ܘܡܫܘܠܬܢܐ ܗܘ *GIWLU*=B u
 ܘܡܫܘܠܬܢ ܗܘ AF s^b
 ܠܒܘܪܐ (2do) *GIWLU*=B
 ܠܒܘܪܢܐ AF s^b
5. ܐܠܐ ܕܬܫܠܡ *GIWLU*=BF s^b
 ܐܠܐ ܬܬܫܠܡ A
9. ܒܡܗܝܡܢܘܬܐ ܗܠܝܢ *GIWLU*=z^2
 ܒܡܗܝܡܢܘܬܐ ܟܠܗܘܢ [A]BF a c r s^b u z^1

I CHRONICLES.

Inscr. ܒܪܝ ܬܪܝܢܕ $GWL =$ BF² a e r s^cer u z
Om. $U =$ AF¹

10. ܫܠܡܗ $GWU =$ [A]BF a s^b z
ܫܠܡܘ L (per errorem)

11. ܒܠܗܬܐ (sine add.) $GWLU =$ B a z
Add. ܘܐܡܪ ܠܗ ܝܒܝܫ ܘܐܪܐ A*F s^cer
(et ver. 12 A*F s^cer). [𝔥 𝔊 q. v.]

15. ܡܨܚܝܠ $GWLU =$ BF a p r [s^cer] u
ܣܡ ܡܨܚܚܠܡ (sic) A

18. ܠܫܝܠܗܝ ܠܗ ܘܐܪܥܐ $GWLU =$ z
Ins. ܥܡ ܟܠܗ ܣܦܐ ܕܠܐ ܡܬܚܫܒ ܐܬܘܐ
ܠܗ ABF a e p r s^b u v

24. ܒܢܘܗܝ ܘܗܠܐ $GWLU =$ B a p u
Praem. ܠܟܘܠܢ ܘܫܠܡܘ AF s^b 𝔥 [𝔊]
ܘܗܠܐ $GWLU =$ [AF ܘܫܠܡܘ] B
ܘܐܪܐ. s^b
𝔥 וגם כל. 𝔊 καὶ (tantum).

25. ܠܚܡ ܠܟܠ $GWLU =$ BF a s^b 𝔥 𝔊
A ܠܟܠ ܗ

30. ܕܒܢܘܗܝ Divisionem in *Libros* ignorant ABF a p
r s^cer u z [C hiat] [Vide ad II. v. 14]

II CHRONICLES.

CHAPTER I. (hiat C)

1. ܕܐܝܣܪܐܝܠ ܟܠܗܘܢ GIVLU=B a p r u
   ܕܐܝܣܪܐܝܠ ܠܟܠܚܕ AF 1 s^b
6. ܒܡܪܝܐ ܕܝܢ GIVLU=z^2 𝕳 𝔊
   ܒܡܪܝܐ ܘܕܝܢ ABF a r s^b z'
7. ܒܠܠܝܐ GIVLU=BF a p s^{cer} u
   ܒܚܠܡܐ (ut 3 Reg. 3. 5. ABN; ܒܠܠܝܐ F) A
10. ܗܢܐ ܗܕܐ ܠܥܡܟ GIVLU=B 𝕳 𝔊
    ܗܢܐ ܗܕܐ ܣܓܝܐ ܗܕܐ ܠܥܡܟ s^b [F om.
    ܗܕܐ 2do]
    ܣܓܝܐ ܗܕܐ ܠܥܡܟ A
12. ܝܗܒܬ ܠܟ ܘܐܡܪ GIVLU=BF a s^b
    ܘܐܡܪ A 𝕳 𝔊
13. ܕܐܘܪܫܠܡ ܟܢܘܫܬܐ ܥܡ ܕܝܢ GIVLU=[B a p r u z$^{1\ ut\ vid}$
    ܡܢ] [s^{cer} ܡܢ] z^2
    ܕܐܘܪܫܠܡ ܟܢܘܫܬܗ ܥܡ F l
    ܠܐܘܪܫܠܡ ܟܢܘܫܬܐ ܥܡ A
    𝕳 ירושלם (tantum), 𝔊 τῆς ἐν Ἱερουσαλήμ.
    ܡܪܟܒܬܐ ܕܝܢ ܥܡ GIVLU=AF 1 s^b z^2 𝕳 𝔊
    Om. ܕܝܢ B a p r u z'
16. ܐܪܡܐ GIVLU=ABF l
    ܐܘܡܢܐ s^{cer}

17. ܘܡ̈ܠܟܐ ܐܕܘܡ. ܘܒܐܝܕܝܗܘܢ ܡܦܩܝܢ *GIVLU* = B [F ܘܠܡ̈ܠܟܐ] s[b]
ܘܠܡ̈ܠܟܐ ܐܕܘܡ ܒܐܝܕܝܗܘܢ ܡܦܩܝܢ (nulla interpunct.) A

Chapter II. (hiat C)

4. [3] ܐܠܗܢ. ܗܕܐ ܠܥܠܡ *GIVLU* = B p u
ܐܠܗܢ ܠܥܠܡ. ܗܕܐ ܠܥܠ AF l s[b] [𝔏 𝔊]
7. [6] ܘܚܟܡ *GIVLU* = B[1] a
ܘܕܚܟܡ AB[2]F l s[b]
14. [13] ܕܐܬܝܗܒ *GIVLU* = B a
ܕܐܬܝܗܒܬ AF s[b]
ܥܡ ܚܟܝ̈ܡܝܟ ܘܚܟܝ̈ܡܘܗܝ, *GIVLU* = B[F om. ܥܡ]
ܥܡ ܚܟܝ̈ܡܝܟ ܘܥܡ ܚܟܝ̈ܡܘܗܝ, A [𝔏 𝔊]
16. [15] ܘܐܝܟ ܡܣܢܝ̈ܩܘܬܟ *GIVLU* = B[F ܡܣܢܩܘܬܟ] s[cer] u
ܘܐܝܟ ܡܣܬܢ̈ܩܘܬܟ A
𝔏 ככל צרכך, 𝔊 *κατὰ πᾶσαν τὴν χρείαν σου.*

Chapter III. (hiat C)

2. ܒܗ ܒܒܢܝܢܐ *GIVLU* = B s[cer] u
ܒܗ ܒܢܝܢܐ AF l
4. ܐܡ̈ܝܢ ܥܣ̈ܪܝܢ (sine add.) *GIV* = z
Add. ܘܪܘܡܗ ܥܣ̈ܪܝܢ ܐܡܝܢ *LU* = ABF s[b]
𝔊[A] (q. v.)
𝔏 (= 𝔊[B]) והגבה מאה ועשרים

II CHRONICLES. 31

8. ܘܩܕܡ ܐܣܬܗ ܚܡܫܝܢ $GWLU=$ B p s^{cer} u 𝔐 𝔊^{A}
   Om. AF 1
   𝔊^{B} καὶ τὸ μῆκος πήχεων εἴκοσι.

   ܚܡܫܝܢ ܥܠ ܐܬܪܐܬܐ ^ ܕܗܒ $GWLU=$ AB s^{b} u
   Ins. ܠܗ̇ܘ F 1
   לכּכּרִים שֵׁשׁ מֵאוֹת (= 𝔊) 𝔐

   ܚܡܫܝܢ (sine add.) $GWLU=$ B p r u
   Add. ܐܪ]ܐܕ F[A ܘܐܪܐ ܠܗܕܒܣܐ ܡܘܪ ܕܣܡ ܗܘܐ s^{b}
   Cf. 𝔐 v. 9b וְהָעֲלִיּוֹת חִפָּה זָהָב, 𝔊 καὶ τὸ
   ὑπερῷον ἐχρύσωσεν χρυσίῳ.

14. ܘܥܒܕ ܫܘܫܠܬܐ ܕܚܒܘܬܐ $GWLU=$ AB s^{b} 𝔐 [𝔊]
    ܘܦܣܩ ܚܒܠܬܐ (tantum) F 1
    וַיַּעַל עָלָיו כְּרוּבִים 𝔐. 𝔊 καὶ ὕφανεν ἐν αὐτῷ
    χερουβείν.

CHAPTER IV. (hiat C.)

5. ܘܗܘܐ ܥܒܝܗ $GWLU=$ B
   ܘܗܘܐ ܥܒܝܗ AF 1 s^{b}
   ܘܐܪܙܐ $GWLU=$ B e p r u z
   ܠܐܪܙܐ AF 1 s^{b}

6. ܠܡܬܐ ^ ܚܕܐ $GWLU=$ B p r u 𝔐 𝔊
   Ins. ܕܢܫܝܐ (ut 3 Reg. 7. 38 ABFN) A*F 1 s^{b}

8. ܦܬܘܪܐ ܥܣܪܐ (sine add.) $GWLU=$ B r
   Add. ܘܣܡ ܐܢܘܢ ܒܗܝܟܠܐ AF 1 s^{b} 𝔐 𝔊
   ܥܫܢܠ ܕܕܗܒܐ ܕܟܝܐ $GWLU=$ BF s^{cer}
   Om. ܕܕܗܒ A 𝔐 𝔊

ܡܐܐ ܘܡܙܪ̈ܩܝܢ (sine add.) *GWLU*=A*B s[b] u
Add. ܐܡܙ̈ܩܝܢ (sic) F l
𝔥 (=𝔊) מאה : ויעש

9. ܕܪܬܐ ܚܕܐ ܪܒܬܐ *GWLU*=BF l s[cer] u
ܚܕܬܐ (pro ܚܕܐ) A [abh. 𝔖 ab 𝔥 𝔊]
ܢܚܫܐ *GWLU*=s[cer] z
ܕܢܚܫܐ ABF l

Chapter V. (hiat C)

2. ܕܐܝܬ ܒܗ̇ *GWLU*=ABF r s[b]
ܕܐܝܼܬ ܒܗ p u
ܕܗܝ ܨܗܝܘܢ *GWLU*=B e p r u z
ܕܗܝ، ܗܝ، ܨܗܝܘܢ AF l s[b] 𝔥 𝔊

3. ܕܡܛܠܠܐ. ܗܘ *GWLU*=BF s[b]
ܕܡܛ̈ܠܠܐ. ܗܘ ܗܘ A

6. ܕܠܐ ܡܬܡܢܝܢ *GW*=BF s[cer]
ܕܠܐ ܡܬܡܢܝܢܐ *L* (sic) [et *U* legens ܥܢ̈ܐ
ܕܠܐ ܡܬܡܢ̈ܝܢܐ ܘܬܘܪ̈ܐ ܕܠܐ ܡܬܚܫܒܝܢ]
ܕܠܐ ܡܢܝܢ A

9. ܘܡܬܚܙܝܢ، ܗܘܘ ܠܒܪ *GW*=z
Ins. ܗܘܘ ܪܝܫܝܗܘܢ ܡܢ ܬܚܝܬ ܡܛܠܬܐ ܠܠܒܪ
ܕܡܫܟܢܐ ܘܠܐ ܡܬܚܙܝܢ *L*[*U* ܠܒܪ ܒܝܬܐ]=
[ABF s[b] ܠܒܪܗ pro ܠܠܒܪ]

10. ܕܟܐܦܐ ܕܦܣܩ *GWLU*=AB e p r s[b] u z
ܕܟܐܦܐ ܕܪܫܡ F l

ܕܗܘܢ *GWL* = B

ܕܗܝ ܗܝ *U* = e

ܗܝ ܗܝ AF 1 s[cer]

14. ܕܫܟܝܢܬܗ *GWU*

ܕܣܟܝܢܬܗ *L* (per errorem)

Divisionem in ܦܠܓܘ̈ܬܐ nullo modo notant AF[1] 1 s[b]

F[2] notam adscripsit quae, nescio cuius manu, erasa est.

ܫܠܡܬ ܦܠܓܘܬܐ ܕܡ (ܡܕܒܪܢܘܬܐ) ܕܣܦܪ ܕܒܪܝܡܝܢ B [e p r u v z] [C hiat]

ܦܠܓܘܬܐ ܐܚܪܝܬܐ ܕܣܦܪ ܕܒܪܝܡܝܢ BC [e p r u v z]

Add. ܬܫܡܫܬܐ C [p ܬܫܡܫ ܕܫܠܝܡܘܢ]

Add. in marg. ܬܫܡܫܬܐ ܕܫܠܝܡܘܢ B e r

Chapter VI.

4. ܒܪܝܟ (sine add.) *GWLU* = z

ܒܪܝܟ ܗܘ ABCF s[b]

13. ܐܣܦܠܐ *GWLU* = r z

ܐܣܦܠܢܐ ABCF s[b]

𝕳 כיור. 𝕲 *βάσιν.*

14. ܕܐܬܝܗܘܢ ܘܫܡܝܐ *GWL*[*U*] = A[C]F 1 s[b] z[2] 𝕳 𝕲

ܕܐܬܝܗܘܢ ܫܡܝܐ B p r u v z[1]

16. ܠܡܗܠܟܘ *GWLU* = BCF s[cer]

ܠܡܗܟܘ A

ܒܢܡܘܣܐ *GWLU*=B r
ܒܢܡܘܣܝ ACF s[cer]
𝔥 בתורתי, 𝔊[B] ἐν τῷ ὀνόματί (νόμῳ 𝔊[A]) μου.

18. [ܒܢܝܢܫܐ] ܥܡ *GWLU*=BCF
ܥܠ A s[b]
𝔥 (=𝔊) את אדם

19. ܐܠܗܐ [ܡܪܝܐ] *GWLU*=B 𝔊
ܐܠܗܝ ACF s[b] 𝔥

20. ܦܬܝܚܢ (sine add.) *GWLU*=z[2]
Add. ܢܗܘܢ ABCF e p r [s[b] ܢܗܘܢ] u v z[1]
ܒܡ̈ܠܝ *GWLU*=[p r u sine sey.] z
ܒܡܠܠ ABCF [s[cer] ܠܡܠܠ]

23. ܟܘܬܗ *GWLU*=B e
ܟܘܬܗܘܢ ACF s[b]

24. ܡܬܬܒܪܝܢ *GW*=z
ܡܬܬܒܪܗ *LU*=B e r
ܡܬܬܒ̈ܪܐ ACF s[b]

31. ܢܕܚܠܘܢ (sine add.) *GWLU*=BC
Add. ܠܟ AF s[b] 𝔥

32. ܪܒܐ (sine add.) *GWLU*=B e p r u v z
Add. ܘܐܝܕܟ ܬܩܝܦܬܐ ܘܕܪܥܟ ܪܡܐ (ut
3 Reg. 8. 42 ABFN) ACF l s[b] 𝔥 𝔊

36. ܟܕ ܢܚܛܘܢ (ut 3 Reg. 8. 46 ABFN) *GWLU*=z[2]
ܡܛܠ (ܡܛܠ) ܕܢܚܛܘܢ ABC e p r s[b] u v z[1]
ܡܛܠ ܕܢܚܛܐ F (cum v. praeced. coniungens)
𝔥 כי יחטאו, 𝔊 ὅτι ἁμαρτήσονται.

CHAPTER VII.

1. ܥ̈ܠܘܬܐ ܘܕܒ̈ܚܐ *GIVLU* = BCF s^cer

ܥ̈ܠܘܬܐ ܘܩܘܕ̈ܫܐ A (cf. 3 Reg. 18. 38 ܘܐܟܠܬ ܥܠܬܐ ܘܩܘܕ̈ܫܐ ABFN)

10. ܒܝܪܚܐ ܕܬܫܪܝ *GIVLU* = B² (B¹ ܬܫܪܝ) CF l s^cer

ܒܝܪܚܐ ܕܬܪܝ A

ܘܒܪܟܘ *GIV* = ABCF e l r s^b z

ܘܒܪܟܗ *LU*

14. ܘܢܬܕܒܪܘܢ *GIVLU* = z

ܘܢܬܕܒܪܘܢ B e p r u v

ܘܢܬܬܒܪܘܢ AC [ܘܢܬܒܪܘܢ F] s^b

𝔐 ויכנעו, 𝔊 *καὶ ἐὰν ἐντραπῇ.*

16. ܘܢܗܘܘܢ *GIVLU* = F l

ܢܗܘܘܢ (sine ܘ) ABC s^b z

18. ܐܫܪܪܝܗܝ *GIVL* = BC²F l z

ܘܐܫܪܝܗܝ *U* = AC¹ s^b

ܥܠ ܟܘܪܣܝܐ *GIVLU* = B p r u z

ܥܠ ܡܠܟܘܬܐ ACF l s^b

21. ܗܟܢܐ ܠܐܪܥܐ ܗܕܐ ܪܒܬܐ: ܘܠܒܝܬܐ ܗܢܐ

GIVLU = BCF l s^b z

ܠܐܪܥܐ ܗܕܐ. ܗܟܢܐ ܘܠܒܝܬ ܗܢܐ A

𝔐 ככה לארץ הזאת ולבית הזה

𝔊 *τῇ γῇ ταύτῃ καὶ τῷ οἴκῳ τούτῳ* (om. ככה)

22. ܘܫܒܩܘ ܠܗܘܢ *GIVLU* = B p u z

ܘܫܒܩܘ ܐܢܘܢ (ut 3 Reg. 9. 9 ABFN) ACF s^b

Chapter VIII.

7. ܕܫܪܟܘ *GIWLU*=BC sᵇ
ܕܫܬܪܟܘ (ut I. vi. 70, ABC) A[F]
𝔥 (=𝔊) הנותר
ܡܢ ܐܡܘܪ̈ܝܐ *GIWLU*=ABC sᵇ
ܕܐܡܘܪ̈ܝܐ F l
13. [ܘܒܫܘܒܚܐ] ܕܟܠ ܝܘܡ *GIWLU*=z² ut vid
ܟܠ ܝܘܡ BC r v z¹ ut vid
ܟܠ ܝܘܡ ܒܝܘܡ AF l sᵇ
𝔥 ובדבר יום ביום, 𝔊 καὶ κατὰ λόγον ἡμέρας ἐν ἡμέρᾳ.
14. ܘܐܩܝܡ ܐܝܟ ܢܡܘܣܐ *GIWLU*=z² 𝔥 𝔊
Om. ܘܐܩܝܡ ABCF e l p r sᵇ u v z¹
15. ܟܗ̈ܢܐ [ܕܦܩܕܗ] *GIWLU*=ABCF 𝔥 𝔊
ܟܘܡܪ̈ܐ sᵇ
18. ܕܝܡܐ [ܐܠܦ̈ܐ] *GIWLU*=BC
ܒܝܡܐ AF sᵇ

Chapter IX.

1. ܕܢܢܣܝܘܗ̄ (2ᵈᵒ) *GIWLU*=z
ܠܢܢܣܝܘܗ̄ ABCF e p r sᵇ u v
2. [ܠܗ] ܟܠܡܕܡ ܘܐܡܪ̈ *GIWLU*=BC p sᵇ u
ܟܘܠ ܡܕܡ ܐܡܪ̈ A
ܟܠܗ ܐܡܪ̈ F l
𝔥 (=𝔊) את כל דבריה (tantum)
ܓܡܠܐ *GIWL*[*U* ܓܡ̇ܠܐ]=[A ܓܡܠܐ] Bᵘᵗ ᵛⁱᵈ C r z
ܓܡ̇ܠ F l [sᵇ ܓܡܠ]

4. ܘܓܘܡܠܐ $GWLU = B$
   ܘܓܡܠܐ ACF [l] s^b
6. ܘܫܬܐ, ܫܬܪ (ut 3 Reg. 10. 7 ABFN) $GWLU = BC$ $p s^b$ 𝔥 𝔊 [ܫܬܪ ܘܫܢܐ (sic) u]
   ܘܫܢܐ ܕܫܬܐ ܫܬܪ AF l
7. [ܗܪܡܪܐ] ܗܢܘ $GWLU = B$ $p u$
   ܗܠܡ ACF s^b 𝔥 𝔊
12. ܠܗ ܘܩܠܐ ܠܗ ܢܣܒ $GWLU = z^2$
    Om. ܠܗ ܘܩܠܐ $ABCF$ $e l p r s^b u z^1$
13. ܟܬܒܬ (sine add.) $GWLU = B$ $p r u z$
    Add. ܣܘ (ut 3 Reg. 10. 14 ABFN) ACF $l s^b$ 𝔥 𝔊
16. ܕܪܚܡܝܢ ... ܡܫܬܡ $GWLU = BC$ z 𝔥 𝔊
    ܦܚܬܡ ... ܕܪܚܡܝܢ AF $l s^b$

CHAPTER X.

1. [3] ܘܐܡܪܝܢ ܐܬܐ $GWLU = B$ $p u$
   [ܐܡܪܐ ܐܬܐ CF $l s^{cer}$] 𝔥 𝔊
   ܐܡܪܐ (tantum) A
4. ܡܒܥܕܗ $GWLU = BCF$ s^{cer}
   ܡܒܥܕܗ A
6. ܐܬܐ ܠ $GWLU = B$ $e p r u z$
   Om. ܠ ACF $l s^b$ 𝔥 𝔊
7. ܘܐܡܪܝܢ ܠܗ $GWLU = B$ r
   ܘܐܡܪܝܢ ܠܗ ACF l [s^b om. ܠܗ]
   ܝܘܡܐ ܠܟܠ $GWLU = BCF$ $e l p r s^{cer} u$
   Om. ܠܟܠ (ut 3 Reg. 12. 7 ABFN) A

9. ܐܢܬܘܢ ܠ *GWLU*=B e p r u z
Om. ܠ ACF l s^b 𝕳 𝕲
ܕܢܗܦܟ *GWLU*=B l p s^{cer} u z
ܘܢܗܦܟ AC
[ܕܢܗܦܘܟ F]
16. ܘܐܡܪܝܢ (sine add.) *GWLU*=B
Add. ܠܗ ACF s^b
17. ܘܕܝܬܒܝܢ *GWLU*=z
Om. ܘ et praem. ܘܒܢ̈ܝ [ܐ]ܝܣܪ[ܐ]ܝܠ (cf. 3 Reg. 12. 17, *L*=ABFN) ABCF e l p r [s^b] u v 𝕳 𝕲

Chapter XI.

9. ܘܣܡ . . . ܣܡ (ut 3 Reg. 12. 29, ABFN) *GWLU*= ABC s^b
ܘܣܡ . . . ܣܡܗ F
10. [17] ܥܓܠܐ (sine add.) *GWLU*=B
Add. ܚܕ (ܚܕ tantum 3 Reg. 12. 30, ABFN) AC [F ܚܕ ܥܓܠܐ] s^{cer}
11. ܩܐܡ ܗܘܬ (sine add.) *GWLU*=e r^1 z
Add. ܫܠܡܐ ABCF r^2 s^b 𝕳 𝕲^{A} (𝕲^{B} vac.)
12. [20] ܘܬܐܙܠܝܢ *GWLU*=ABC e s^{cer}
ܘܐܢ ܬܐܙܠܝܢ F l
ܚܠܐ *GWLU*=A$^{ut\ vid}$ B [C sine puncto] F l
ܘܚܠܐ s^{cer}
14. ܠܘܬܟ (ut 3 Reg. 14. 6, ABF[N]) *GWLU*=B
ܠܟ ACF s^b 𝕳 אֵלֶיךָ, 𝕲 πρὸς σέ.

Chapter XII.

13. ܘܥܒܬܒܗܪ̈ܐ *GIVLU*=B
    ܘܥܒܒܗܪ̈ܐ AC[F add. sey.] s^b

14. ܠܡܒܥܝܘܗܝ *GIVLU*=B e
    ܠܡܬܒܥܘܗ ACF s^b

Chapter XIII.

4. [ܛܘܪܐ] ܡܢ *GIVLU*=BCF e l p u z
    ܥܠ A s^{cer}
    𝔐 מעל להר צ', 𝔊 ἀπὸ τοῦ ὄρους.

5. ܕܡܠܚܐ [ܩܝܡܐ] *GIVLU*=ABC z
    ܕܡܠܝܚܐ F s^b
    𝔐 מלח, 𝔊 τοῦ ἁλός.

11. ܢܛܪ̈ܝܢ *GIVLU*=BC e s^b u
    ܢܛܪܢ F l
    𝔐 שמרים אנחנו, 𝔊 φυλάσσομεν ἡμεῖς.

ܢܛܘܪ̈ܬܗ *GIVL*=B l u
    ܢܛܘܪܬܗ̈ *U*=[C ܢܛܘܪ̈ܬܐ] F s^b

15. ܬܒܪ *GIVL* [*GIV* ܬܒ݂ܪ]
    ܬܒܪ *U*=BCF e [s^b ܬܒ݂ܪ] z

17. ܐܢܘܢ [ܘܚܪܒ] *GIVLU*=BC p s^b u z
    ܒܗܘܢ F l
    𝔐 ויכו בהם, 𝔊 καὶ ἐπάταξεν ἐν αὐτοῖς.

ܪܒܐ [ܚܪܒܐ] *GIVLU*=B p u z
    ܪܒܬܐ CF s^b

18. ܣܘܡܕܢ GWLU = BCF   s^b u
    ܕܚܠܠܝܗ p
    𝔥 נשענו, 𝔊 ἤλπισαν.
    ܚܠ ܡܢܝܐ (sine add.) GWLU = B   u
    Add. ܗܡ CF   s^b

Chapter XIV. (hiat A)

5. [+] ܐܡܪܘ GWLU = BC   p s^{cer} u
   ܐܡܪܒܝ F   1
   𝔥 ויסר, 𝔊 καὶ ἀπέστησεν.
   [ܘܕܒܚܐ] ܢܟܣܬܐ GWLU = BC   p s^{cer} u
   ܕܢܒܚܐ F
   𝔥 הבמות, 𝔊 τὰ θυσιαστήρια.

[9. [8]] ܠܗܡ ܡܠܟܐ ܘܡܪܟܒܬܐ GWLU = BC[F ܐܪܒܥ]
   s^b
   𝔥 (= 𝔊) ומרכבות שלש מאות]

11. [10] ܘܣܡܟ GWLU = B   r
    ܗܘܣܡ (absque ܘ) CF   1 s^b
    ܐܠܗܢ ܡܢܝ GWLU = z
    ܐܠܗܢ ܡܢܝ BCF   e p r [s^b ܐܠܗܢ ܐܡܢܝ] u v
    𝔥 יהוה אלהינו, 𝔊 Κύριε ὁ θεὸς ἡμῶν.
    ܐܬܬܟܠܬ ܠܐ GWLU = BC   r v
    ܐܬܬܟܠ ܠܐ F   s^b

13. [12] ܩܠܐܘܣ (sine add.) GWLU = B   𝔊
    Add. ܕܢܓܠ CF   s^b 𝔥

Chapter XV. (hiat A)

12 (item 14). ܘܣܒܘ GWLU = B   p u
    ܘܣܒܪܐ CF [s^b ܘܣܒܘ]

17. ܦܘܪܣ [ܠܟܐ] *GWLU*=CF sᵇ [u]
ܦܘܪܣܘܣ B p
ܒܪܡ ܠܗܘܢ *GLU*=BC
ܡܛܠ ܕܠܗܘܢ F

18. ܘܩܘܕܫܐ ܕܐܒܘܗܝ ܠܒܝܬܗ [ܕܡܪܝܐ] *GWLU* = z²
(z¹ om. ܕܐܒܘܗܝ)
ܘܩܘܕܫܘܗܝ، ܠܒܝܬܗ (ut 3 Reg. 15. 15, ABFN)
sᶜᵉʳ
ܘܩܘܕܫܐ ܕܒܝܬܗ BCF e l p r u v

Chapter XVI. (hiat A)

1. (ܘܫܢܬ) ܫܢ̈ܬ (sine add.) *GWLU*=B e z 𝔓
Add. ܬܡܢ CF l sᵇ
ܠܡܦܩ ܘܠܡܥܠ *GWLU*=BF e l 𝔓 𝔊
ܠܡܥܠ ܘܠܡܦܩ C sᶜᵉʳ

3. ܡܬܠܟܐ *GWLU*=BCF z [Cf. I. xxi. 22, *L*=z]
ܕܡܬܠܟܐ sᶜᵉʳ

4. [ܫܬܠܟܐ] ܠܒܪ *GWLU*=B p u z
ܠܒܪ̈ܘܢ CF l sᵇ

11. ܗܐ ‸ ܟܬܝܒܝܢ *GWLU*=B p u z
Ins. ܗܢܘܢ CF l sᵇ 𝔓

12. ܘܐܬܟܪܗ . . . ܘܐܬܟܪܗ *GWLU*=BC e p sᵇ u z
[1]ܘܐܬܟܪܗ . . . ܘܐܬܟܪܗ (sic) F d l m

Chapter XVII. (hiat A)

16. ܐܠܦܝܢ ‸ ܕܫܠܚܐ *GWLU*=B p u
Ins. ܫܠܝܚܐ CF l sᵇ 𝔓 𝔊

[1] Add. ܡܢ ܪ̈ܓܠܘܗܝ، d m (et F l ?)

Chapter XVIII.

(A hiat; v. 19b—29a desid. apud C)

1. ܣܟܠ GWLU = B
   ܣܟܠܗܘܢ CF 1 s[b]

5. ܢܬܒ (ut 3 Reg. 22. 6, ABF[1]N) GWLU = BF 1 p u 𝕳 𝔊
   Add. ܐܠܗܐ s[cer]
   ܐܝܟܠ C[ut vid]

12. ܐܠܗܐ ܢܬܒܗ (ut 3 Reg. 22. 13, ABN; om. ܐܠܗܐ F) GWLU = BC e p s[cer] u z
    ܐܢܬܒܗ ܚܕܐ F d l m

13. ܐܡܪܐ (2[do]) GWLU = B p u
    ,ܐܡܪ CF s[b]

16. ܡܕܒܪܝܢ GWLU = B p u
    ܡܕܒܪܝܢ (sine ܘ) CF s[b]

33. ܕܘܪܟܒܬܐ GWLU = BC e p s[cer] u 𝕳 𝔊
    Om. F d l m
    (ܕܘܪܟܒܬܐ post ܡܠܟܘܢܐ 3 Reg. 22. 34, ABFN)

Chapter XIX.

4. ܐܒܗܬܗ GWLU = B e p u
   ܐܒܗܬܗܘܢ CF 1 s[b] 𝕳 𝔊

10. ܘܗܐ GWLU = B p u 𝕳
    (ܗܐ) ܗܠ CF s[b] 𝔊

---

[1] ܢܬܒܗ F

Chapter XX.

16. ܘܗܘܢ *GWLU*=B p u
ܗܘܢ (sine ܘ) ACF s^{b}

17. ܘܐܕܝܢ ܡܪܐ ܡܪܘܬܐ *GWL*=B e z
ܘܐܕܘܢ ܡܪܐ ܡܪܘܬܐ *U*=AC p s^{b} u [F ܡܪܝܐ
tantum = 𝔍 𝔊]
ܒܒܕܪܘܢ *GWLU*=B e
ܒܘܒܕܪܘܢ ACF s^{b}

Chapter XXI.

4. ܒܚܪܒܐ *GWLU*=ABCF e
ܒܘܐܪܣܐ s^{cer}

Chapter XXII.

1. ܡܫܪܝܬܐ ܕܐܫܡܥ[ܐ]ܠ *GWLU*=BC p u
ܡܫܪ̈ܝܬܐ ܒܐܘܪܫܠܡ s^{cer}
ܡܫܪ̈ܝܬܐ (sine add.) A[F sine sey.] 𝔍

2. ܥܣܪܝܢ ‸ ܘܬܪܬܝܢ *GWLU*=BF l
Ins. ܗܘܐ AC s^{b} [B, non F, ins. ܗܘܐ post
ܥܣܪܝܢ]

3. ܡܛܠ ܕܒܪ ܚܬܗ ܗܘܐ ܕܐܚܐܒ *GWLU*=BC p s^{cer} u
ܡܛܠܠ ܕܒܪ ܚܡܬܗ ܗܘܐ ܕܐܚܐܒ A
ܡܛܠ ܕܒܪܬ ܚܬܗ ܕܐܚܐܒ ܡܬܐ ܗܘܬ ܠܗ F l
Abhorret 𝔖 ab 𝔍 𝔊

II CHRONICLES.

4. ܟܕܒܠܝܗܘܢ ܳ *GWLU*=B   p u
   ܟܕܒܠܚܬܗܘܢ A   s^{cer}   [ܟܕܒܠܬܗܘܢ F]
   ܟܕܒܠܐܚܕܗܘܢ C

6. ܕܒܪܟܘܡ, *GWLU*=BCF   s^b
   ܕܒܪܘܡ, (ut 4 Reg. 8. 29, ABFN) A
   ܟܪܘܝܠܐ (sine add.) *GWLU*=B
   Add. ܗܘܐ ܝܗܘܕܐ ܠܚܡܐ (cf. 4 Reg. 8. 29
   ܗܘܐ ܝܗܘܕܐ, ABFN) ACF   s^b

11. ܕܒܟܪܝܐ [ܟܠܘܐܚܒ] (ut 4 Reg. 11. 2, ABFN)
    GWLU=BCF   s^{cer}
    ܕܒܟܪܘܡ A

Chapter XXIII.

1. ܘܠܡܟܪܐ *GWLU*=ABC   p s^b u
   ܘܠܟܡܪܐ F   d m   [𝔐 fere ac 𝔊 מעשיהו]

3. ܟܢܘܫܬܐ *GWLU*=CF
   ܟܢܘܫܬܐ (sine ܒ) A   [s^{cer} add. sey.]
   ܟܢܘܫܬܐ B (sed ver. 2 ܟܢܘܫܬܐ ut C)

4. ܕܗܘܪܝܢ *GWLU*=B
   Praep. ܕ ACF   s^b

11. ܟܠܗܝܢ ܝܗܒ *GWLU*=BCF   p s^{cer} u
    Ins. ܒ A
    ܟܪܘܙܘܐ *GWLU*=B   e p z   [u ܟܪܘܙܘܐ]
    ܟܪܘܙܘܐ ACF   l s^{cer}

12. ܟܬܝܒ *GWLU*=B   p u
    ܕܢܫܒܚ ACF   s^b

14. [ܟܬܒܘܗܝ] ܒܝܕ GWLU = BF p u
    ܒܝܕܘܗܝ AC s^cer
    [ܐܝܬܗ] ܠܐ GWLU = BCF s^cer
    ܕܠܐ A
18. ܥܒܕܝܗܘܢ GW = z
    ܥܒܕܝܗܘܢ LU = ABCF p s^b u 𝔐 𝔊
19. ܕܣܓܝܐܝܢ (sine add.) GWLU = ABC p s^b u
    Add. ܠܣܝܒܘ F d l m
    [ܢܚܠܘܢ] ܕܠܐ GWLU = B
    ܘܠܐ ACF s^b
20. ܘܣܥܕ GWL = z
    ܘܣܥܕܗ U = ABCF s^b

Chapter XXIV.

1. ܥܬܕ ˰ ܥܢܡ GWLU = BCF z
   Ins. ܗܘܐ A s^b
   ܘܥܒܝܐ (ut 4 Reg. 12. 1, ABFN) GWLU = BC z
   ܘܥܒܝܐ A s^b   𝔐 [𝔊 'Αβιά = עביה]
   ܘܥܒܝܐ F d l m
5. ܘܫܕܪ ܟܢܫ GWLU = B e p u z
   Om. ܟܢܫ ACF 1 s^b   [𝔐 𝔊 vac.]
6. ܡܛܠ GWLU = BCF 1 s^cer u z [ראש 𝔐 fere ac 𝔊]
   ܟܢܫ A e p
7. ܚܟܡ GWLU = B e p u z
   ܬܠܡ ACF 1
   ܚܠܡ s^cer

II CHRONICLES.

18. ܪܒܝܐ ܐܬܒܘܐ *GWLU*=BCF 1 s^cer z 𝔇
    ܪܒܝܐ (tantum) A 𝔊
23. ܦܐܡܪܝܢ *GWLU*=BF z 𝔇 𝔊
    ܦܐܡܪܝܐ AC s^b
24. ܡܐܟܠܐ *GWLU*=BCF p s^cer u
    ܡܐܟܠܐ A
    ܐܚܘܗܝ *GWLU*=z (ܐܚܘܗܝ)
    ܐܚܘܗܝ ABCF p s^b u
27. ܣܓܕ [ܕܒܢܣܬ] *GWLU*=BCF 1 p s^cer u z
    ܪܒܘܬ A

Chapter XXV.

6. ܪܐܡܝܢ *GWLU*=BCF
   ܪܐܡܝܢ A s^b
9. ܐܠܗܐ [ܢܬܠ] *GWLU*=BC s^b
   ܢܐܠܟ AF
11. ܪܓܒܐ (sine a) *GWLU*=z
    Praem. a ABCF s^b
15. ܪܒܝܐ [ܕܒܚܬܐ] *GWLU*=BCF s^cer
    ܪܒܝܐ ܡܠܟܝ A
16. ܕܒܝܬܐ ܪܒܠܫܢ *GWLU*=BC s^b
    ܕܒܝܬܐ ܪܒܠܫܢ [A] F 1 [A add. ܡܠ]
    [ܕܫܪܐ] ܪܒܐ *GWL*=z
    ܪܒܐ U
    ܪܒܐ ABCF e l p r s^b u v
19. ܢܦܠ ܒܝ *GWLU*=AB[C] p s^b u

ܐܬܬܪܝܡ ܠܒܟ (cf. 4 Reg. 14. 10[1] ܘܐܪܝܡܟ ܠܒܟ
ABN) F

ܡܬܪܥܪܥܬ *GWLU*=ABC $s^b z^2$ [u ܐܢܬ ܡܬܪܥܪܥܬ]
ܡܬܪܥܪܥܬ F p z^1
Cf. 4 Reg. 14. 10 ܘܠܐ ܬܬܪܥܪܥ [A]BN

ܥܠ ܒܝܫܬܐ *GWLU*=BCF p s^{cer} u
ܠܒܝܫܬܐ (ut 4 Reg. 14. 10, ABN) A

ܕܬܦܠ *GWLU*=z^2
ܘܬܦܠ (ut 4 Reg. 14. 10, ABN) AF s^b
ܘܕܬܦܠ BC p u z^1

ܘܥܡܟ [ܝܗܘܕܐ] *GWLU*=B p u
ܘܕܥܡܟ AC[F ܘܥܡܟ] s^b

28. ܘܩܒܪܘܗܝ (sine add. ut 4 Reg. 14. 20, ABN) *GWLU*
=p u [z ܘܩܒܪܘ]
Add. ܒܩܒܪܗܘܢ ABCF l s^b

Chapter XXVI.

3. ܐܟܠܝܐ *GWLU*=BC p s^{cer} u z
ܡܚܝܠܐ (ut 4 Reg. 15. 2, N. ܐܡܚܝܠܐ AB) A
ܢܟܠܝܐ F l
𝔥 (Ḳri) יכליה

16. ܐܬܬܪܝܡܬ (sine add.) *GWLU*=B p u
Add. ܠܗ CF l
Add. ܗܘܬ ܠܗ A s^b

[1] Desid. 4 Reg. 13. 13b—16. 19a apud F

20. ܟܘܪܐ *GWLU*=ABC p u

ܟܪܝܐ F l s^{cer} 𝔏 [𝔊 vac]

ܘܪܒܐ ܕܟ̈ܗܢܐ *GWLU*=z^2

ܘܟܠܗܘܢ ܟ̈ܗܢܐ ABCF l p s^b u 𝔏 [𝔊 vac.]

21. ܕܚܒܫܘܬܐ [ܚܒܝܫܬܐ] *GWLU*=z^2

ܕܚܒܫܬܐ ABCF e l p r s^b u z^1

Chapter XXVII.

2. ܠܐ [ܥܠܡܘܕ] *GWLU*=z^2

ܕܠܐ ABCF p s^b u z^1

4. ܘܡܘܪ̈ܝܐ *GW*=ABCF s^b z

ܡܘܪ̈ܝܐ (sine ܘ) *LU*

5. ܘܡܙܒܘ [ܣܥܒܘ] *GWLU*=z

ܕܡܙܒܘ [A]BCF e p r s^b u v

Chapter XXVIII.

9. [ܠܥܒܪܝܡ] ܘܐܬܐ *GW*=z

ܕܐܬܐ *LU*=ABCF e p r s^b u v

ܕܐܒ̈ܗܬܢ *GWLU*=B e p r u v z

ܕܐܒܗܬܗܘܢ AC s^b

ܕܐܒܗܬܟܘܢ F

13. ܬܘܒ ܣܓܝܐ *GWLU*=BCF e s^{cer} z

Om. ܬܘܒ A 𝔏

16. ܠܡܥܕܪܘܬܗ *GWLU*=B p u v z 𝔏 𝔊

Praem. ܠܡܐܬܐ ACF l s^b

17. [ܝܗܘܕܐ] ܒܚܒܝܬ *GWLU*=BF p u v z
ܕܝܚܒܝܬ AC
ܠܝܚܒܝܬ s[cer]

18. ܘܠܓܙܪ *GWLU*=e z 𝔊[B]
Praem. ܘܠܬܡܢܐ ܘܠܟܠܐ̈ܚܬܗ ABCF l p s[b] u v
𝔍 (=𝔊[A]) ואת תמנה ואת בנותיה

19. ܕܐܚܙ *GWLU*=F z
ܕܚܙܘ ABC e s[b] v

21. ܒܬܪ̈ܐ [ܘܡܟ̈ܬܐ] *GWLU*=BCF v [ܘܡܟܒܬ F]
ܕܒܬܪ̈ܐ A s[b]

23. ܠܝܗܘܕܐ ˰ ܘܐܚܪܒ *GWLU*=z
Ins. ܢܦܫܗ ܘܐܚܪܒ ABC[F] c l p r s[b] u v
[F ܠܢܦܫܗ]

25. ܕܒܚ̈ܐ *GWLU*=p u v z
ܡܕܒܚܐ ABCF l s[cer]
ܠܡܕܒܚܘ *GWLU*=B p u v z
ܠܡܚܠܨ ACF l s[b]
ܕܒܚ̈ܐ ܠܡܕܒܚܘ pro לקטר במות 𝔍 (=𝔊)

27. ܕܐܝܣܪܝܠ [ܕܡܠܟ̈ܐ] *GWL[U]*=BC [s[b]] v 𝔍 𝔊
ܕܝܗܘܕܐ AF

CHAPTER XXIX. (a *ver.* 5 hiat C)

1. ܚܙܩܝܐ ܗܘ ܒܡܠܟܘܬܐ *GWLU*=BC p [s[cer]
ܘܚܙܩܝܐ] u v 𝔍 𝔊
Om. AF l
ܒܥܣܪ̈ܝܢ ˰ ܘܚܡܫ *GWLU*=BCF p s[cer] u v
Ins. ܗܘܐ A

9. [ܢܦܠܘ] ܘܗܐ *GWLU*=B p s^cer u v z 𝔥 (והנה נפלו)
ܘܗܫܐ AF l
ܘܒܢܬܗܘܢ ܘܒܢܝܢ *GWLU*=B p u v
Praem. ܘܢܫܝܢ A s^b
Add. ܘܢܫܝܢ F

22, 23. ܟܗ̈ܢܐ ܘܩܪܒܘ ‸ .ܕܡܕܒܚܐ *GWLU*=
AB p u v 𝔊^B
Ins. ܘܢܟܣܘܢ ܐܡܪ̈ܐ ܘܢܬܘܢ ܕܡܗܘܢ
.ܥܠ ܩܪ̈ܢܬܐ ܕܡܕܒܚܐ [F] s^cer 𝔥 𝔊^A
[ܐܡܪ̈ܐ ܘܢܬܘܢ ܕܡܗ F]

36. ܕܡܢ ܥܠ *GWL*=B p r u v z
ܕܡܢ ܥܠ *U*=[ܘܡܢ A] s^cer
(ܡܢ ܥܠ ܗܘܐ ܦܬܓܡܐ F l)

Chapter XXX. (hiat C)

1. ܠܦܨܚܐ (sine add.) *GWLU*=B p u v 𝔥 𝔊
Add. ܫܠܝܚܬܐ AF l s^b
2. ܘܐܬܡܠܟ *GWLU*=z^2
ܘܐܬܚܫܒܘ A[F] [l] [s^cer]
ܟܢܘܫܬܐ [ܘܟܠܗ] *GWLU*=z^2 𝔥 𝔊
ܥܡܐ AF l s^b
Add. ܕܐܝܣܪܐܝܠ ܘܗܘܘ AF s^b
Hunc versum (nisi verba ܒܝܪܚܐ ܬܢܝܢܐ) B e p r u v z^1 prorsus om. Habent AF s^cer z^2
6. ܘܒܦܘܩܕܢܐ *GWLU*=B p u v
ܒܦܘܩܕܢܐ AF l s^b

II CHRONICLES.

ܘܡܣܒܝܢ $GWLU=$ B p u   [𝕳]
ܘܡܣܒܐ AF s[b]   𝕲[A]

8. ܡܪܠܚܐ $GWLU=$ BF p s[cer] u   𝕳 𝕲[A]
ܠܚܕܐ A   [𝕲[B]]
ܙ.ܡܐܟܪܙ $GWLU=$ B s[cer] u
ܙ.ܡܐܟܪܙ [A ܐܙ.ܡܐܟܪܐ] F p

9. [ܠܬܬܚܐ] ܡܕܡ $GWLU=z^2$ 𝕳 𝕲[A]
ܠܚܡ ABF e p r s[b] u v

14. ܟܬܝܬܐ (sine add.) $GWLU=z^2$ [𝕳]
Add. ܟܝܘܬܐ.ܬ AF s[cer]   [𝕲 q. v.]
ܒܢܝܘ $GWLU=z^2$
ܢܝܘܒ AF s[cer]
Post ܟܬܝܬܐ hiant B a e p r u v z[1]   usque ad
ver. 22 (ܚܕܬ ܡܫܚܐ)

16. ܟܐܒܪ (1mo) $GWLU=$ F
ܟܐܒܪ A s[b]

18. ܘܒܝܣܐ ܠܐ.ܬ $GWLU=$ AF 1
ܘܒܝܣܐ ܠܐ.ܬ s[cer]

21. ܐܘܚܕܐܟܬ ܠܗܘ $GWLU=$ F z^2
Om. ܠܗܘ A s[b]   𝕳 𝕲
ܟܬܘܙܚܐܒ ܟܠܡܐܗ $GWLU=$ F 1 [s[cer] sine ܒ]
ܟܬܘܗܙܚܒ ܟܠܡܐܗ A

CHAPTER XXXI. (hiat C)

1. ܟܬܝܬܐ ܢܝܡܪܐ $GWLU=$ B p u
Ins. ܢܝܡܪܐ ܟܡܪܒܐ AF s[b]

4. ܕܢܣܒ [ܡܛܠ] *GWLU*=AB
ܕܢܣܝܒ F^ut vid^ l

5. ܐܦܫܛ *GWLU*=z²
ܦܫܛ ABF l s^b v z¹ [ܘܟܕ ܦܫܛ ܦܬܓܡܐ
ܦܫܛ ܟܕ ܐܝܣܪܝܠ F l]

10. ܘܦܪܐ *GWLU*=B^ut vid^ p u z
ܘܐܡܪ AF s^b 𝔥 𝔊 (vide infra)
ܘܐܡܪ ܠܗܘܢ *GWLU*=[A ܠܗ] B p u [𝔥 𝔊^B]
Om. F s^b 𝔊^A (vide supra)

16. [ܫܢܝܢ] ܬܠܬ *GWLU*=BF p s^cer^ u 𝔥 𝔊
ܬܠܬܝܢ A

Chapter XXXII. (hiat C)

1. ܘܩܘܫܬܐ (sine add.) *GWLU*=B a p r u
Add. ܗܠܝܢ AF l s^b 𝔊
𝔥 הדברים והאמת האלה

4. ܕܡܠܟܐ ܢܐܬܐ *GWLU*=B [F l ܕܕܡܠܟܐ] p s^cer^ u
ܠܐ ܢܐܬܐ A
𝔥 למה יבואו, 𝔊 μὴ ἔλθῃ.

7. ܘܐܬܬܥܫܢܘ [ܐܬܠܒܒܘ] *GWLU*=B p s^cer^ u z
ܘܐܬܥܫܢܘ AF l 𝔥 𝔊
[ܕܡܢ] ܥܡܢ *GWLU*=B [F l om. ܕܡܢ] p u
ܕܥܡܢ A s^b 𝔥 𝔊

9. ܡܢ ܒܬܪ *GWLU*=z 𝔥
ܘܡܢ ܒܬܪ ABF p [r] s^b u v 𝔊

12. ܐܥܒܪ ܚܙܩܝܐ *GWLU*=BF p [s^b] u
ܐܝܢܐ ܗܘ ܚܙܩܝܐ A

II CHRONICLES.

14. ܐܡܪ̈ܝܢ ܓܒ ܂ ܡܬܚܙܝܢ̈ GWLU = BF p u z
    Ins. ܕܡܣܬܥܪ̈ܢ ܒܪ̈ܙܐ ܠܓܒܗ̇ܕܐ A s^{cer}
    [𝔏 𝔊]
16. ܗܘܐ ܟܠܗ GWLU = BF s^b
    Om. ܗܘܐ A
17. ܐܠܗܐ̈ܬ ܘܕܒܚ GWLU = z²
    ܘܕܒܚ ܘܐܠܗܐ̈ [AF ܕܘܒܚ] B a p r s^b u v
    𝔏 𝔊
    ܠܓܒܗܘ GWLU = z
    ܠܓܘܣܘܐ (ut 4 Reg. 19. 4, 16 ABFN) ABF
    a e p r s^b u v
    ܡܬܚܙܝܢ̈ ܓܒ ܐܡܪ̈ܝܢ (sine add.) GWLU = B
    a e p r u v z
    Add. ܐܘ ܠܐܒܗܘܟ ܕܠܐ ܒܪ̈ܝܐ ܠܓܒܗ̇ܕܐ ܣܠܩܘ
    ܡܬܚܙܝܢ̈ ܡܢ ܐܡܪ̈ܝܢ AF s^{cer} (ܘܐܒ) [𝔏 𝔊]
22. ܕܐܒܗܬܗܘܢ GWLU = B
    ܕܐܒܗܬܗܘܢ AF [s^b ܕܐܒܗ̈ܬܗܘܢ]
25. ܘܡܠܟܐ̈ ܕܐܚܐܒ ܐܚܐܒ GWLU = z²
    Om. ܐܚܐܒ ABF a e p r s^b u v z¹
26. ܠܡܠܟܐ ܕܐܬܟܬܒ̈ ܒܐܦܠ (= ver. 25) GWLU = z²
    (z¹ hiat)
    ܠܡܠܟܐ̇ ܒܚܙܘܐ ABF a e l p r s^b u [v ܒܚܙܘܐ
    sine ܒ]
    𝔏 בְּגֻבַּהּ לִבּוֹ, 𝔊 ἀπὸ τ. ὕψους τ. καρδίας αὐ.
27. ܘܚܛܗܘܗ̈ GWLU = B p r s^b u v z 𝔏 [𝔊]
    ܘܚܛܗܘܗ̈ F l
    ܘܚܛܗ̈ܘܗܝ A

ܟ̈ܠ ܪܓܝܓܬܐ *GIWLU*=B p r u v z

ܪܓܝܓܬ ܪܓܝܓܬܐ A s[b] [F l ܟܠ ܪܓܝܓܬܐ]

ולכל כלי חמדה 𝔥

30\. ܡܦܩܢܐ ܕܡ̈ܝܐ ܕܓܝܚܘܢ ܠܥܠܝܬܐ *GIWLU*=AB s[b] u

ܡܦܩܢܐ ܕܡܝܐ ܕܬܚܬܝܬܐ F (cf. Is. 22. 9 *L*= ABCF)

ܠܡܥܪܒܐ *GIWLU*=BF u

ܠܡܥܒܐ A [s[b] ܠܡܥ̈ܪܒܐ] [𝔥 𝔊]

ܡܕ̈ܢܚܐ *GIWLU*=BF s[cer] u 𝔥 𝔊

ܡܕܢܚܐ A

32\. ܒܣܦܪܐ *GWL* [ܘܒܣܦܪܐ *U*]=z

Praem. ܐܦ A l

" ܘܐܦ BF e p r s[cer] u v

Chapter XXXIII. (hiat C)

2\. ܕܐܘܒܕ *GIWLU*=z[2]

ܕܒܕܪ ABF e l p r s[b] u v

3\. ܘܒܢܐ ܡܕ̈ܒܚܐ ܕܒܕܪ *GIWLU*=BF l p s[cer] u

𝔥 𝔊

ܘܒܕܪ ܡܕܒܚܐ ܕܒܢܐ A

ויבן את הבמות אשר נתץ 𝔥

ܘܣܓܕ ܠܟܠܗܘܢ *GIWLU*=B p u

ܘܠܟܠܗܘܢ (om. ܣܓܕ) AF l s[b]

11\. ܒܫܘ̈ܫܗܝ *GIWLU*=AB p s[b] u

ܒܫܠܕܘܗܝ F 𝔥 בחוחים

13\. ܒܡܠܟܘܬܗ *GIWLU*=v z

ܠܡܠܟܘܬܗ ABF p r s[b] u

II CHRONICLES.   55

14. ܥܡ ܡܚܕܐ ܕܚܣܢܐ $GWLU = \mathrm{B[F]}$ p s^cer u
    ܥܡ ܡܚܕܐ ܠܚܣܢܐ A (𝔐) (מערבה לגיחון)
16. ܕܒܝܬܐ $GWLU = \mathrm{B}$ p r s^cer u v z
    ܕܒܝܬܚܐ AF 1   𝔐 𝔊
17. ܐܚܠܬܐ $GWLU = z$
    ܐܚܠܬ ܠܗ ABF l p r s^b u v
19. ܐܠܗܐ܊ ܡܚܠܨܐ $GWLU = \mathrm{B}$ e p u z
    ܘܐܠܗܐ A [F l sine ܘ] s^b
    ܘܡܢ ܥܡܐ $GWLU = \mathrm{B}$ e p u
    ܘܡܢܗ ܥܡܐ AF s^b

Chapter XXXIV. (hiat C)

5. [ܐܦ] ܥܠܝ $GWLU = \mathrm{B}$ [F s^cer ܥܠ] a p u z
   ܥܠܘܗܝ A
17. ܘܣܡ (sine add.) $GWLU = z$
    Add. ܠܗ ABF e p r s^b u v
21. ܡܕܡ ܕܟܬܝܒ $GWLU = \mathrm{BF}$ s^b   𝔐 𝔊
    ܡܕܡ ܐܡܪ A
22. ܫܒܢܐ [ܒܪ] $GWLU = \mathrm{B}$ e p u z
    ܫܒܢܐ (ut 4 Reg. 22. 14 ABFN) AF s^b
    𝔐 בן חסרה (Chron.), בן הרחס (4 Reg. 22. 14)
26. ܘܥܠ ܡܠܟܐ $GWLU = \mathrm{B}$ 𝔊 (καὶ ἐπί)
    ܘܠܡܠܟܐ AF s^b   𝔐 (ואל)
30. ܘܐܠܗܐ $GWLU = z^2$ 𝔐 𝔊^A [ܘܐܠܗܐ F]
    ܐܠܗܐ AB^{ut vid} p s^cer u v z^1
31. ܘܐܝܟܢܐ (sine add.) $GWL[U] = z$ 𝔐 𝔊
    Add. ܗܘܐ ABF p s^b u v

33. ܘܝܩܪ̈ ܟܠܗ ܥܡܐ *GWLU*=p [s^cer ܘܝܩܪܘܗ] u v
ܘܝܩܪܘܗ ܟܘܠܗ ܥܡܐ A [B neq. legi]
ܘܝܩܪܘܗ ܠܝܩܪܗ F

Chapter XXXV. (hiat C)

1. ܕܐܪ̈ܡܣܒܪܐ *GWLU*=B [p] u
ܒܐܪܡܣܒܪܐ AF s^b 𝔏 𝔊

3. ܠܟܘܢ ܬܘܡ *GWLU*=p u v z
ܠܟܘܢ ܬܘܒ AB^ut vid F s^b

6. [ܕܡܠܠ] ܐܚ̈ܝܟܐ *GWLU*=BF p s^b u
ܦ̈ܘܡ A
ܥܡ ܡܘܫܐ *GWLU*=BF z [𝔏 𝔊]
ܥܡ ܐܚܝ̈ܟܘܢ A s^b

8. ܘܪ̈ܘܪܒܢܘܗܝ *GWLU*=B p u [𝔏 𝔊]
ܘܕܪܘܪ̈ܒܢܘܗܝ AF s^b [F punct. post ܠܥܡܐ]
ܫܠܡܝܐ *GWLU*=BF p s^b u [𝔏 𝔊]
ܠܫܠܡܝܐ A
ܠܟܗܢܐ. ܥܢܐ ܐܠ̈ܦܐ ܬܪܝܢ ܘܫܬܡܐܐ ܘܬܘܪ̈ܐ
ܬܠܬܡܐܐ *GWLU*=B e p u [𝔏 𝔊]
ܠܟܗܢܐ ܐܠ̈ܦܐ ܬܪܝܢ ܘܫܬܡܐܐ. ܘܬܘܪ̈ܐ[1]
ܬܠܬܡܐܐ. AF s^b

11. ܘܙܪܩܘ *GWLU*=u z
ܘܐܙܪܩܘ ABF p s^b v

18. [ܐܬܥܒܕ] ܘܠܐ *GWLU*=B p u 𝔏 𝔊
ܕܠܐ AF s^b

---

[1] Sine sey. F.

II CHRONICLES.

21. ܠܡܚܣܘܠܗܘܢ $GWLU = F$ e p s^b u v
    ܠܡܚܣܘܠܗ, A
    ܡܢ ܐܠܗܐ ܕܚܡܬ ܘܕܐܠܟ ܒܣܘܠܡ $GWLU = A$
    ܚܡܕ. ܐܠܗܐ ܕܚܡܬ ܠܟ ܒܣܘܠܡ BF p s^b u v
23. ܐܚܙܝܗܘ ܡܠܟܐ $GWLU = B$ e p u v
    Ins. ܠܚܬܪܗܘ, AF s^{cer} 𝔓 𝔊
    [A ܐܚܙܝܗܘ,]
24. ܡܢ ܚܙܝܬܗ $GWLU = BF$ e p s^b u v
    ܡܢ ܗܘܝܐ A
    ܚܙܝܘܗܝ $GWLU = AF$
    ܗܘܝܐ B e p s^b u v
25. ܚܦܣܝ $GWL = B$ e p u v
    ܚܦܣܝ $U = AF$ s^b

CHAPTER XXXVI. (hiat C)

1. ܟܣܐ (sine add.) $GWLU = B$ p u
    Add. ܟܐܪܝ, AF s^b 𝔓 𝔊
10. ܝܠܗܘܡ, ܝܫܪ $GWLU = A$ a^2 e p^2 [s^b ܡܠܝܢ] u v
    [B periit]
    Om. ܝܠܗܘܡ, F a^1 p^1 𝔓 𝔊
14. ܠܗܠ ܡܥܬܐ $GWLU = F$ p u v z 𝔓
    Om. ܠܗ A s^b
15. ܘܡܣܥܕܝ $GWLU = AF$ s^b v
    ܘܡܣܥܕܝ e p u$^{ut\ vid}$
    ܠܥ ܕܢܗܝܪ $GWLU = B$ e p u
    ܠܥ ܕܟܠܝ, AF s^b

B.   8

18. ܐܘܒܠܗ *GWLU*=B p u
ܐܘܒܠ AF sʰ

23. ܕܢܒܝܐ [ܐܠܗܐ] *GWLU*=BF c p sʰ u
ܡܪܬܝܐ A

COLOPHON.

A ܫܠܡ ܟܬܒܐ ܕܣܦܪ ܕܒܪܝܡܝܢ ܘܕܝܘܡܕܐ (sic)

ܫܠܡ ܣܦܪ ܕܒܪܝܡܝܢ ܕܐܝܬܘܗܝ ܦܘܠܓܐ ܬܢܝܢܐ
ܐܠܦܝܢ ܘܫܬܡܐܐ ܘܬܠܬܐ [B] c p r u v z

F ܫܠܡ (tantum)

ܫܠܡ ܟܬܒܐ ܕܣܦܪ ܕܘܟܪ ܢܩܦܬܐ ܕܡܠܟܐ ܕܝܘܡܕܐ
ܕܒܝܬܡܘܪܐ ܣܦܪ ܕܒܪ ܢܒܝܢ ܀ s^cer

INDEX.

The following are the most important or most interesting words found in the variations from the printed text. The word used in the printed text is appended in curved brackets. Verbs are cited in the voices in which they occur.

ܐܠܗܡ (ܠܕܬܝܢ)	I. XXIII. 4.
ܐܡܛܠܐ (ܐܡܛܠܐ)	II. VI. 13.
ܐܟܪܙ aphel (ܐܟܪܙ)	II. XIV. 5.
ܐܬܒܪ v. ܐܬܬܒܪ (ܐܬܒܪ)	II. VII. 14.
ܐܬܕܫ (ܐܬܕܫ)	I. XII. 8.
ܐܬܕܫܘ (ܐܬܕܫ)	II. XVI. 12.
ܐܬܕܫܢ (ܐܬܕܫ)	II. XXXII. 7.
ܐܬܬܠܬܠ (ܐܬܠܬܠ)	II. XXV. 19.
ܐܬܬܒܪ See ܐܬܒܪ	II. VII. 14.
ܒܩܣܡܐ	II. XXXI. 1.
ܒܩܣܡܐ (ܒܠܩܛܐ)	II. XIV. 5.
ܒܠܢܝ (ܒܚܡ)	II. XXIV. 7.
ܠܓܐ (ܠܓܒܐ)	II. XXXII. 30.
ܕܢܪܡܝܡ	I. XXVII. 24.
ܗܦܟܝ (ܗܦܟܝ)	I. IX. 1.
ܠܬܗܦܟܘ—ܗܦܟܝ	II. VI. 16.

ܚܕ — ܚܕܐ	II. IX. 13 & XI. 10.
ܚܕܘܬܐ (ܚܕܝܘܬܐ)	II. XXVI. 21.
ܚܕܬܐ (ܚܕܐ)	II. IV. 9.
ܚܘܕܐ (ܚܘܕܪ̈ܐ)	II. XXIII. 11.
ܚܠܦ (ܚܠܛ)	II. XXXIV. 5.
ܚܡܬܐ	II. XXII. 3.
ܚܣܕ (ܚܣܪ)	II. XXXII. 17.
ܚܪܒ [ܒܗܘܢ]	II. XIII. 17.
ܛܝܒܘܬܐ (ܚܣܕܐ)	I. XIX. 2.
ܛܥܡܐ (ܛܥܡ)	I. IV. 41.
(ܝܩܝܪܐ — ܝܩܝܪ̈ܐ)	I. XIII. 8.
ܝܕܥ	II. VI. 20.
ܝܗܝܒܘܬܐ (ܝܗܒܐ)	II. XXXII. 30.
ܝܬܪ (ܝܬܪ)	II. VIII. 7.
ܝܬܒ (ܝܬܒ)	I. X. 7.
ܟܪܣ (ܟܪܣ)	II. XXX. 9.
ܡܟܝܪ̈ܐ *v.* ܡܟܝܪܘܬܐ (ܡܟܝܪܐ)	II. XXXII. 27.
ܡܕܒܪ[ܕ] (ܡܕܒܪܢܐ)	I. XVIII. 15.
ܡܛܠ (ܡܛ)	II. VI. 36.
ܡܠܟܐ (ܡܠܟܐ)	II. XIII. 5.
ܡܪܕܘܬܐ (ܡܪܘܬܐ)	II. X. 4.
ܡܥܒܕܢܐ (ܡܪܐ)	I. VI. 32.

INDEX.

(ܒܚܠܐ) See (ܡܚܠܐ)	I. XIII. 8.
ܨܡܕ (ܥܡܠ)	I. XVIII. 7.
ܣܘܡܐ (ܣܘܢܩܐ)	I. XVI. 3.
ܣܥܪܐ (ܣܥܪܬܐ)	II. IX. 16.
ܚܠ (ܚܡ)	I. XIX. 2 & II. VI. 18.
,, (ܡ)	II. XIII. 4.
ܚܡܝ (ܐܡܪ)	II. XXXIII. 2.
,, (ܒܝܢ)	II. XXX. 14.
ܩܠܥܐ (ܡܚܠܐ)	I. XIII. 8.
ܥܕܪ (ܚܕܪ.)	I. XVII. 10.
ܦܒ (ܒܦ)	I. XIV. 11.
ܣܘܬܐ (ܣܕܬܐ)	I. XX. 3.
ܥܠܝ (ܛܥܢ)	I. V. 1.
ܩܒܠ ܣܡ ܒܠܐ	II. XI. 11 (cp. I. XII. 1).
ܩܕܝܪܐ (ܣܕܪܐ)	I. XII. 8.
ܩܠ ܛܠ (ܚܠ)	I. XVIII. 10.
ܩܦܣܐ (ܕܣܐ)	II. VII. 1.
ܪܓܠܐ (nom. to ܐܬܪܓܠ)	II. XXV. 15.
ܪܘܚ (ܢܘܚ)	I. IV. 9.
ܪܗܛܐ	II. XXXII. 26.
ܪܥܝ (ܣܡ)	II. V. 10.

INDEX.

ܫܘܼܚܬܐ (ܫܘܼܚܬܐ)   II. xxx. 21.
ܫܘܥ (ܫܘܥ)   I. xx. 5.
ܫܡ [ܡܢ] (ܫܡ ܡܢ)   II. xxix. 36.
ܫܡܐ ܫܬܐ (ܫܬܐ)   I. xi. 20.
ܫܬܐ (ܫܬܐ)   I. xxi. 5.
ܫܬܝ (ܫܬܝܬ)   II. vii. 10.

ܫܪܬܐ (ܫܪܬܐ)   II. xxxiii. 16.

INDEX OF PASSAGES REFERRED TO ON TEXTUAL GROUNDS.

	PAGE		PAGE
Gen. x. 4 (bis), 14 (bis), 22	1	3 Reg. XII. 7	37
XXXVI. 35	2	17, 29, 30	38
XLIX. 4	4	XIV. 6	38
1 Sam. XVII. 7	15	XV. 15	41
XXXI. 2, 7 (bis)	5	23	Addenda
2 Sam. III. 3	2	XVIII. 38	35
5	3	XXII. 6, 13, 34	42
V. 8	6	4 Reg. VIII. 29 (bis)	44
VI. 19	9	XI. 2	44
VII. 3	10	XII. 1	45
8	11	XIII. 13—XVI. 19	47 note
VIII. 2, 6, 7, 10	12	XIV. 10 (quater), 20	47
16	13	XV. 2	47
X. 2, 3, 5	13	XIX. 4, 16	53
16, 19	14	XXII. 14	55
XXI. 19	15	Is. XIII. 22	xix
XXIII. 8 (bis), 13	6	XVI. 1	xix
21	7	XXI. 9	xix
XXIV. 13	15, 16	XXII. 9	54
18, 21	16	Jer. VI. 1, 6	xix
3 Reg. III. 5	29	XVII. 1	xix
V. 11	2	XVIII. 23	xix
VII. 38	31	Ezek. VI. 14	xix
VIII. 42, 46	34	XXVI. 17	xix
IX. 9	35	(For other references to Ezekiel	
X. 7, 14	37	see Introduction, pp. xxiii—xxvi.)	

CAMBRIDGE: PRINTED BY J. AND C. F. CLAY, AT THE UNIVERSITY PRESS.

www.ingramcontent.com/pod-product-compliance
Lightning Source LLC
Chambersburg PA
CBHW032242080426
42735CB00008B/970